AF248363

Soul Made Whole:

Healing the Wounds Within

David Webb

Printed in the United States of America

First Printing: 2026

Eternal Kingdom International Publishing, LLC

LIBRARY OF CONGRESS

LCCN: 2026940837

ISBN- 978-1-968815-21-9 - Paperback

ISBN- 978-1-968815-20-2 - eBook

ISBN- 978-1-968815-22-6 - Hardcover

A Note from EKI Publishing:

This book is part of a larger Kingdom reading pathway developed through EKI Books. These works are designed to help readers grow from foundational truths into mature Kingdom life, moving from repentance, identity, and inner restoration into transformation, body life, leadership, and deeper revelation. While each book may be read on its own, together they form a broader discipleship framework.

The EKI Reading Pathway

Foundations
- *Repent: U-Turns Required* - Kirkland M. Rite *(Coming Soon)*
- *Baptized: Why Did I Get Wet* - Kirkland M. Rite
- *Sozo: What Am I Saved From* - Kirkland M. Rite *(Coming Soon)*

Identity
- *Unchained* - Kirkland M. Rite

Discern the Times & Understand His Voice
- *The Language of Dreams (title forthcoming)* - David S. Webb *(Coming Soon)*
- *I Am the Sign* - Kirkland M. Rite *(Coming Soon)*

Restore the Inner Life
- *Soul Made Whole* - David S. Webb *(Coming Soon)*

Grow Into the New Nature
- *The New Nature Series* - Kirkland M. Rite *(Coming Soon)*

Walk in Kingdom Life
- *Walking in the Kingdom* - David S. Webb *(Coming Soon)*
- *Escape the Shame of Babylon* - David S. Webb
- *The Unique Factor* - David S. Webb

Build Within the Body
- *Building the King Through the Local Church* - David S. Webb
- *Building the Temple to Hold the Glory* - David S. Webb
- *Every Joint Supplieth* - Kirkland M. Rite *(Coming Soon)*

Multiply and Lead
- *Spiritual Fathers (title forthcoming)* - David S. Webb *(Coming Soon)*
- *The Elisha Mandate* - Kirkland M. Rite *(Coming Soon)*

Go Deeper
- *A Gospel of Convicts* - Kirkland M. Rite *(Coming Soon)*
- *The Covenant of Salt* - Kirkland M. Rite *(Coming Soon)*

Foundational and Supplemental Works
- *The Noah Generation* - Kevin Rice
- *Cultivating the New Nature: Growing into the Full Stature of Christ* - Kevin Rice

Companion Resources
- *Values for Living Above and Beyond* - Kevin Rice *(Coming Soon)*

Workbooks and Study Guides - EKI Publishing Team *(Coming Soon)*

Other Works by David S. Webb:

- *Escape The Shame of Babylon* EKI Publishing 2025

- *The Unique Factor* EKI Publishing 2025

- *Building the Kingdom Through the Local Church* EKI Publishing 2025

- *Building the Temple to Hold The Glory* EKI Publishing 2026

http://www.DavidSWebb.com

The Spirit of the Lord is upon me... to heal the brokenhearted... to set at liberty them that are bruised.

-   Luke 4:18 (KJV)

Dedication:

"For which of you, intending to build a tower, sitteth not down first, and counteth the cost, whether he have sufficient to finish it."
    - Luke 14:28 (KJV)

This book is dedicated to my family, friends, mentors, and pastors who have walked with me through the seasons of life, stood with me in hard places, and helped shape the man I became in God.

This book, like all the books I have written, came at a cost. The Scripture says to count the cost. In my case, there was no long season to sit back, measure it slowly, or prepare my heart for what was coming. I was thrust into circumstances that forced me to learn quickly, deeply, painfully, and permanently. I was taken into lessons I never would have chosen for myself, and yet those lessons marked me forever.

I went kicking and screaming into the things that taught me what fills these pages. I resisted what I did not understand. I wrestled with what I did not want. I was changed by fires I did not ask for, and by roads I would not have chosen. But when the time came to leave that season, I found that what once broke me had also taught me, and what once wounded me had also prepared me. I did not want to leave, because I knew I was leaving with something costly, something holy, and something meant to be given away.

So I took what I learned in that season and shared it with those God placed in front of me. And for those I could not reach in time, for those I had to leave behind when another season called my name, I wrote this book. These pages carry the weight of experience, the burden of truth, and the mercy of lessons learned under pressure.

This book is for those who needed it when I was there, for those I was able to help, and for those I could not reach before God moved me forward. It is my prayer that what cost much to learn will become grace to receive, healing to the wounded, light to the hidden places, and strength to every soul that reads it.

Contents

Prelude

The Soul Must Be Restored

Introduction: Salvation Is Not the End of the Matter

There is a lie many believers live under without realizing it.

They assume that because they are born again, everything inside them must already be functioning the way it should. They assume that because their spirit came alive to God, their soul must also already be whole. They assume that because they love Jesus, the inward fractures, the old reactions, the damaged interpretations, the hidden fears, the bruised memories, the crooked appetites, and the mixed responses no longer matter.

But that is not true.

The moment you get born again, you are a new creature, but your soul is still carrying many of the same things it was carrying before you were saved. Your spirit may belong to God, but your mind, will, emotions, conscience, personality, memory, and inward habits still have to be brought under His rule. That is where much of the Lord's work in your life actually happens. The soul is where so many of the battles are felt, so many of the lies are believed, so many of the wounds are carried, and so much of life is interpreted.

"And the very God of peace sanctify you wholly; and I pray God your whole spirit and soul and body be preserved blameless unto the coming of our Lord Jesus Christ." (1 Thessalonians 5:23, KJV)

If Scripture speaks of spirit, soul, and body distinctly, then they are not all the same conversation.

That means salvation and soul restoration are not identical subjects.

You can be genuinely saved and still have a bruised soul.

You can love God and still have damaged reactions.

You can belong to Christ and still need the inward life restored.

"He restoreth my soul: he leadeth me in the paths of righteousness for his name's sake." (Psalm 23:3, KJV)

If the soul needs restoring, then the soul can be damaged.

And if the soul can be damaged, then the church must stop pretending that everybody who is saved is automatically whole.

This book is about that restoration.

Spirit • Soul • Body

1 Thess. 5:23 • "I am a spirit. I have a soul. I live in a body."

You Are a Spirit, You Have a Soul, You Live in a Body

If you do not understand what you are, you will misread what is happening inside you.

You are a spirit. You have a soul. You live in a body.

The soul is not your spirit, and it is not your body. It is the inward life through which you think, choose, feel, remember, imagine, react, and interpret. It is where your mind operates, where your will agrees or resists, where your emotions rise and fall, where your conscience either stays tender or becomes dull, and where your personality expresses what has been shaping it.

Your body is not neutral. It carries appetite, impulse, craving, instinct, and reaction. Your flesh does not care whether you go to heaven or hell. There is no plan of salvation for your flesh. It does not care. That is why the body was never meant to rule you. And the plan is for you to be able to control it after encountering Jesus. But later, to get a new body.

"For our conversation is in heaven; from whence also we look for the Saviour, the Lord Jesus Christ: Who shall change our vile body, that it may be fashioned like unto his glorious body..." (Philippians 3:20–21, KJV)

And your soul stands in the middle of these realities. It is where so much of the battle is actually experienced.

Wounds vs. Scar vs. Stronghold

Wound	Scar	Stronghold
Still open Still reactive Easily triggered Pain rises fast Needs healing	Healed but remembered No longer ruling Can be touched without controlling your response	Damage is organized into a pattern False belief system Reaction becomes a habitual rule

Not every damaged area is the same

A wound needs healing
A stronghold is damage
that has built a false pattern of
thought and response

Psalms 147:3
2 Chorithinas 10:4-5
Hebrews 12:15

That is why the logos matters so much. The written Word of God separates a person's soulish part from their spiritual part. It exposes what is truly under God and what is still being ruled by something else. It shows what conviction is and what is mere reaction. It reveals what is spiritual hunger and what is fleshly appetite. It helps a person stop calling damage maturity and stop calling confusion personality.

"For the word of God is quick, and powerful, and sharper than any twoedged sword, piercing even to the dividing asunder of soul and spirit..." (Hebrews 4:12, KJV)

That verse is one of the keys to this whole book.

The soul and spirit are not the same thing.

And if the Word must divide them, then many people have been living blended where God intended separation.

The Soul Is Where Life Gets Interpreted

You do not live life directly out of your spirit.

You do not live life straight out of your body either.

You live it through your soul.

That means if the soul is damaged, life gets misread.

If the soul is wounded, relationships get misread.

If the soul is bent, correction gets misread.

If the soul is cluttered, perception gets cluttered.

If the soul is restricted, the flow of God through a person gets restricted.

That is why two people can hear the same truth and walk away with completely different reactions. One hears mercy. Another hears rejection. One hears correction. Another hears attack. One hears love. Another hears control. One hears wisdom. Another hears oppression.

The issue is not always the truth they heard.

The issue is often the soul through which it was being processed.

That is also why many people are not meeting the real you.

They are interacting with your soul damage.

They are meeting your bruise, your fear, your hidden shame, your learned reactions, your old agreements, your unhealed history, and the inward places that still have not been brought into truth. What should be flowing cleanly through you gets colored by what the soul is still carrying.

That is devastating because it is true.

But it is also hopeful.

Because what can be identified can be healed.

The Word of God Is the Maintenance Plan for the Soul

One encounter is not a maintenance plan.

A new car may come off the lot with a full tank, but nobody with sense believes that one tank was meant to carry the vehicle for life. When that fuel runs out, maintenance stops being optional. It becomes required. The soul works the same way.

Many people want one altar, one service, one touch, one emotional breakthrough, one season of help, or one powerful meeting to do what only daily bread can do. But God did not design the inward man to live on yesterday's fuel.

"But he answered and said, It is written, Man shall not live by bread alone, but by every word that proceedeth out of the mouth of God." (Matthew 4:4, KJV)

"Give us this day our daily bread." (Matthew 6:11, KJV)

If man must live by every word, then daily bread is not optional.

It is maintenance.

It is not religious routine.

It is not a hobby for intense believers.

It is not a private preference.

It is maintenance for sanity.

Presence without Word produces instability. A person can feel God in a room and still think crooked the next morning. They can speak in tongues and still answer life from damage. They can cry in a service and still have an unrenewed mind. That is why the soul must be restored through ongoing feeding, not only through momentary encounter.

"And be not conformed to this world: but be ye transformed by the renewing of your mind..." (Romans 12:2, KJV)

Renewing is not a one-time event.

Renewing is ongoing resistance against drift.

Sheep Eat Slow

God did not call His people sheep by accident.

Sheep eat slow.

That is why God gave repeated witness in the Word instead of assuming one pass would fix everything in your soul. Sheep are ruminants. Sheep have four sections in their stomach. They do not swallow once, process once, and move on. They take in what they are fed, and then they keep working it through. They take in a mouthful of grass or grain, and it goes into the first chamber where it begins to be broken down. Then they bring it back up and chew it again. Then it is distributed into the second chamber. They repeat that process into the third chamber, and by the fourth chamber it goes out. That is how sheep eat. They eat slow. They process by repetition. They work it over again and again until it has fully moved through them.

That is why God gave four Gospels telling the same Christ from different angles.

Not because heaven was empty of content.

Because sheep eat slow.

People often mistake recognition for digestion. They hear a truth once, nod at it, and assume they possess it. But hearing is not digestion. Agreement is not incorporation. Recognition is not embodiment. The soul often has to hear truth, receive truth, chew truth, revisit truth, and let truth move through layer after layer until what was once merely heard becomes part of the inward man.

"As newborn babes, desire the sincere milk of the word, that ye may grow thereby." (1 Peter 2:2, KJV)

Growth is tied to intake.

Some people are not rebellious in every area.

They are under-chewed.

Intelligent but Ignorant

There are many people who are intelligent but ignorant.

Intelligent means they have capacity.

Ignorant means they do not actually know because they have never been exposed, never read, never fed, never worked the truth through, and never let it become part of their inward structure. How can a person know what they never read? How can they stand on what they never fed on? How can they call themselves stable while ignoring the very book God gave for their edification?

That is why underfed souls become unstable souls.

Without daily bread, the mind becomes foggy. Affection becomes misplaced. Perception becomes dull. Judgment becomes unreliable. People begin calling bondage freedom, appetite identity, preference discernment, and damage wisdom. They may remain religious. They may remain vocal. They may remain involved. But they become less sane because the inward man is not under sufficient truth to stay ordered.

The written Word of God was designed for your edification.

It was designed to shape, sand, turn, and work things in you until it becomes easier to relate rightly to God, rightly to people, and rightly to truth.

"All scripture is given by inspiration of God, and is profitable... That the man of God may be perfect, throughly furnished unto all good works." (2 Timothy 3:16-17, KJV)

A Restored Soul Can Carry More of God

If the soul is not restored, it limits how much of God can flow through you.

That does not mean you are less saved.

It means you can become less sane, less clear, less stable, less perceptive, less responsive, less able to receive, less able to discern, and less able to carry what heaven is trying to pass through the inward man.

A damaged soul can keep a person from expressing how God actually made them. It can shut down personality, joy, courage, healthy expression, and normal relationship. It can make people interact not with the real you, but with your damage. What they are meeting is not your healed self, but your injured reactions. Not your restored personality, but your wounded responses.

Damage vs. Personality

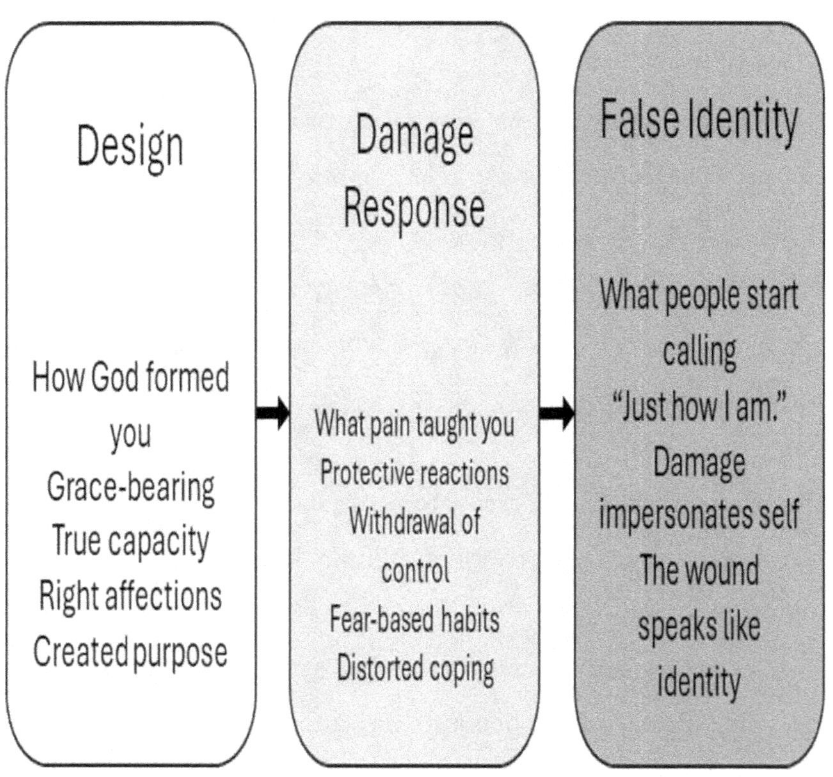

Healing separates who God made you
from what damaged trained you
to become

PSALMS 139:14
ROMANS 12:2
EPHESIANS 4:22-24

That is why soul restoration is not a side issue.

It affects everything.

It affects your relationship with truth.

It affects your relationship with people.

It affects your ability to perceive danger and receive promise.

It affects how the river of God comes through your life.

Conclusion: The Soul Must Be Restored

This book begins here because everything else depends on it.

The soul must be restored.

Not merely inspired.

Not merely comforted.

Not merely impressed.

Not merely touched in moments.

Restored.

That means the hidden places must come into the light. That means the Word must divide soul from spirit. That means daily bread must become non-optional. That means the mind must be renewed, the affections reordered, the conscience kept tender, the reactions retrained, and the inward life brought back under the government of Christ.

"Create in me a clean heart, O God; and renew a right spirit within me." (Psalm 51:10, KJV)

"Behold, thou desirest truth in the inward parts..." (Psalm 51:6, KJV)

God does not merely want your attendance.

He wants truth in the inward parts.

He wants a soul that can receive, process, respond, and carry life rightly.

He wants to restore what sin damaged, what fear bent, what culture dulled, what appetite distorted, what false religion shut down, and what darkness taught the soul to tolerate.

The Shepherd still restores souls.

And if the soul is restored, life stops being interpreted by damage and starts answering to truth.

Scripture Index:

- Matthew 4:4
- Matthew 6:11
- Romans 12:2
- 1 Thessalonians 5:23
- 2 Timothy 3:16-17
- Hebrews 4:12-13
- Psalm 23:3
- Psalm 51:6
- Psalm 51:10
- 1 Peter 2:2
- 2 Corinthians 6:11-12
- Psalm 119:11
- Psalm 119:105

Part I

The Soul Under Assault

The soul is not damaged by accident. It is struck, bent, trained, bruised, and taught. Long before the wound is explained, it is already being lived. Long before the damage is named, it is already talking through fear, appetite, hiding, anger, shame, and disorder. This opening movement does not flatter the reader. It diagnoses the inward fracture. It exposes the animal nature, the residue of sin, and the reason so many people love God yet still answer life from bruising instead of wholeness. Heaven is not insulting the wound. Heaven is locating it. What can be named can be targeted. What can be targeted can be restored.

"And the very God of peace sanctify you wholly; and I pray God your whole spirit and soul and body be preserved blameless unto the coming of our Lord Jesus Christ." (1 Thessalonians 5:23, KJV)

Chapter One

You Are More Than What You Feel

Introduction: The Battle Begins in the Unseen Man

Most people are losing battles they do not even know they are fighting.

They think the problem is outside them, so they keep changing scenery while the same inward fracture follows them from room to room, church to church, season to season, reaction to reaction, and disappointment to disappointment. They change settings and keep the same torment. They change language and keep the same bondage. They change routines and keep the same private contradiction. Why? Because the deepest battle of your life does not begin around you. It begins in the unseen man.

This generation desperately needs an eternal perspective. You are a spiritual being having an earthly experience, and you are just passing through. All through Scripture, the Shepherd keeps moving His people through crossings, wildernesses, process, and transition. They were never meant to build permanence out of what they were only called to pass through. If you get too permanent on earthly things, you will miss heavenly things. And that is part of the bondage of this age. The world trains people to chase the next new thing. It makes what you have feel old the moment something newer appears. A man can have five phones that still work and still want another one, not because the old one failed, but because his soul has been trained to crave novelty. But when you get Jesus Christ, there is no next version. We do not need a new Jesus. We need understanding saints.

One of the first lies that must die is the lie that your feelings are your truest self. They are not. Feelings are real, but they are not qualified to rule you. They can report trouble without diagnosing it. They can be intense and still be wrong. They can be sincere and still be deceived. If you build your life on sensation, you will misread yourself, misread God, misread people, and misread the war taking place inside you.

"But man is born unto trouble, as the sparks fly upward." (Job 5:7, KJV)

God is not trying to help you feel better inside disorder. He is after truth in the inward parts (Psalm 51:6). He is after wholeness. He is after an inward life that can carry His rule without twisting it. That is where this book must begin.

You Are a Spirit, You Have a Soul, You Live in a Body

If you do not understand what you are, you will misread everything happening inside you.

You are a spirit. You have a soul. You live in a body (1 Thessalonians 5:23). And if you want the blunt version, you are a spirit, you have a soul, and you live in an animal body. That language rubs proud people the wrong way, but pride does not get to rewrite reality. Scripture is not embarrassed by creaturely language. Romans 8:21 speaks of "the creature" being delivered from the bondage of corruption into the glorious liberty of the children of God (KJV). Genesis 9:15 speaks of *"every living creature of all flesh"* (KJV). Ezekiel saw living creatures moving with the Spirit of God, and *"the spirit of the living creature was in the wheels"* (Ezekiel 1:20, KJV; Ezekiel 10:20, KJV). Heaven is not trying to insult you. Heaven is trying to humble you enough to diagnose you.

"And the very God of peace sanctify you wholly; and I pray God your whole spirit and soul and body be preserved blameless unto the coming of our Lord Jesus Christ." (1 Thessalonians 5:23, KJV)

"Because the creature itself also shall be delivered from the bondage of corruption into the glorious liberty of the children of God." (Romans 8:21, KJV)

Your body is not neutral. It carries appetite, impulse, instinct, craving, and reaction that were never meant to sit on the throne. Your flesh does not care whether you go to heaven or hell. Why? Because there is no plan of salvation for your flesh. It does not care. It wants relief, gratification, indulgence, stimulation, and immediate response. It wants what it wants, when it wants it, and it wants your whole life arranged around feeding it. That is why Scripture says the law is spiritual, but man in himself is carnal (Romans 7:14), and the carnal mind *"is enmity against God"* (Romans

8:7, KJV). If the body rules, appetite rules. If appetite rules, discernment dies. If discernment dies, life gets animal fast.

"For we know that the law is spiritual: but I am carnal, sold under sin." (Romans 7:14, KJV)

"Because the carnal mind is enmity against God: for it is not subject to the law of God, neither indeed can be." (Romans 8:7, KJV)

That is why the cross is not decoration. It is not jewelry. It is not a religious logo. It is the instrument by which the beast gets judged. The cross is not for your boss. The cross is not for your pastor. The cross is for that animal nature in you that does not want the rule of Christ. It is there to kill the beast.

You do not live life straight out of your body or straight out of your spirit. You live it through your soul. You think through your soul, interpret through your soul, attach through your soul, react through your soul, remember through your soul, and receive through your soul. So when the soul is damaged, life is misread. When the soul is cluttered, perception is cluttered. When the soul is wounded, relationships are wounded. When the soul is ungoverned, life becomes unstable. Too many people stop at experience and never deal with condition. They know how to shout, know how to survive a service, know how to wear a church version of themselves, and still have an inward man that has never been brought into order.

Dead Men Do Not Eat

The soul cannot stay healthy without daily feeding.

Jesus said, *"Man shall not live by bread alone, but by every word that proceedeth out of the mouth of God"* (Matthew 4:4, KJV). He also taught us to pray, *"Give us this day our daily bread"* (Matthew 6:11, KJV). Every living thing must be fed.

That line is simple, but it is devastating.

Every living thing must be fed.

A number of years ago, a man was selling shoes. He said he was a Christian, but he also admitted he never really read his Bible. Then he asked the question that opened the door: why did he not read the Bible more? The answer came back sharp and clean: dead men do not eat.

That got his attention.

It hit him hard enough that what should have been a quick exchange turned into about an hour-long conversation about the Bible, spiritual life, and what it means to actually live from the Word of God. Years later, he still stays in touch. Why? Because truth landed with force. It did not flatter him. It woke him up.

Dead men do not eat.

You can set the finest meal in front of a corpse, and nothing will happen. You can put the best bread in the room, open the Bible, preach pure truth, and still get no response if life has gone dull inside. The issue is not the quality of the bread. The issue is whether the inward man is alive enough to hunger.

"But he answered and said, It is written, Man shall not live by bread alone, but by every word that proceedeth out of the mouth of God." (Matthew 4:4, KJV)

"Give us this day our daily bread." (Matthew 6:11, KJV)

That is the condition of many believers. Bread is present. Truth is present. The Word is present. But the inner man is so underfed, so underdeveloped, and so disconnected that he has little appetite for what would actually make him whole.

And if you are not eating your daily bread, guess what part of you most people are running into?

Animal nature.

That is why somebody can have a fish on the back of the car, then curse in traffic like hell is in the driver's seat. The fish is not the issue. The issue is starvation. They are not always fake Christians. Many times they are undernourished Christians. They have enough religion to identify with church and not enough inward life to answer pressure like Christ. The spirit is neglected, the soul is unrenewed, and the animal nature keeps taking the microphone.

That phrase needs to stay with the reader: undernourished Christians. It explains far more than most people think. It explains why truth feels distant, why appetite for the Word disappears, why private reactions stay ugly, and why people can look religious while living mostly out of flesh, habit, offense, and impulse. Dead men

do not eat. And if the inward man is not being fed, something else
will rise and rule.

The Soul Is the Battlefield of Your Life

The soul is not static. It is not parked. It is not frozen in
place. It is always being shaped upward toward order or downward
toward distortion (Romans 12:2). Your soul condition can go up,
and your soul condition can go down. You can be cleaner than
you were, or more cluttered than you were. More whole than you
were, or more mixed than you were.

That is why the soul is the battlefield of your life. It is
where truth and lies collide. It is where memory fights meaning. It
is where what God says crashes into what damage says. It is where
conviction and excuse meet each other. It is where the war over
government is actually felt.

*"And be not conformed to this world: but be ye transformed by the
renewing of your mind, that ye may prove what is that good, and acceptable,
and perfect, will of God."* (Romans 12:2, KJV)

Scripture calls one form of that division double-
mindedness.

A double minded man is unstable in all his ways." (James 1:8,
KJV)

Two opposing ideas in the same soul do not make
you deep. They make you unstable. You do not get one mind for
prayer and another for lust, one mind for worship and another for

self-protection, one mind for Scripture and another for rebellion. You get one heart, one mind, one will. And when those are split against themselves, the soul begins to crack.

That is why the Word of God must cut where your excuses blur. Hebrews 4:12 says the Word is living and sharp, piercing even to the dividing asunder of soul and spirit. The Word exposes what is spiritual and what is soulish. It reveals what is conviction and what is reaction. It separates what your wound is saying from what God is saying. It cuts mixture. Many people do not want that sword. They want comfort without cutting, healing without exposure, power without order, and freedom without diagnosis. But God does not heal dishonestly. He heals where truth is allowed to pierce.

"For the word of God is quick, and powerful, and sharper than any twoedged sword, piercing even to the dividing asunder of soul and spirit..." (Hebrews 4:12, KJV)

You Let the Wrong Thing Name You

Most people misread themselves because they judge themselves by sensation instead of truth.

I feel peace, so God must be in it.

I feel angry, so I must be right.

I feel empty, so something outside me must fill me.

I feel numb, so maybe nothing is wrong.

No.

Feelings are signals. They are not thrones.

A person can feel peace and still be deceived. A person can feel troubled and actually be under conviction. A person can feel strong and really be hardened. A person can feel numb and call that maturity when it is actually deadness. Dullness is not peace. Shutdown is not wisdom. Deadness is not balance. And right-feeling is not the same as right.

"There is a way which seemeth right unto a man, but the end thereof are the ways of death." (Proverbs 14:12, KJV)

Most people do not know how much of what they call personality is really untreated damage. They react and call it discernment. They withdraw and call it wisdom. They go numb and call it peace. They defend themselves and call it strength. But hiding is not identity. Many times it is just the soul backing away from exposure.

That is also why people begin overstimulating the body when the soul grows dull. They are trying to feel through the flesh what was designed to be alive in the soul. So they overdo everything. More stimulation. More appetite. More distraction. More noise. More excess. But counterfeit intensity never heals the wound. It only deepens the need. If the soul is not ruled, the body will start volunteering substitutes.

Do Not Let Animal Manifestation Push You Out of the Kingdom

One of the strongest warnings in this whole message is this: do not let animal manifestation in God's people push you out of the Kingdom.

Some people were stronger in soul three years ago than they are now. Then they got angry, got bitter, got offended, and let somebody else's animal manifestation become the excuse for their own inward decline. Somebody in church acted all animal, and instead of judging it correctly, they started blaming the Kingdom itself.

That is foolish.

Sometimes church people really do act all animal. Sometimes you get more animal than Christ on a particular Sunday. Sometimes a pastor has an animal manifestation. Sometimes a leader has an animal manifestation. Sometimes a religious nutcase, a foolish pastor, or a church hypocrite makes a complete mess. But do not let somebody else's untransformed soul become your permission slip to stop eating spiritual food. Do not let damaged people push you away from the only river that can heal what they aggravated.

Think about Noah in the ark. If it was not for the storm on the outside, he could not have handled the stink on the inside. That is part of church life too. Sometimes the ark smells like animals because there are still animals inside it. But the stink inside does not make the ark false. It only proves you are still traveling with creatures who need transformation.

So judge it right.

Do not call the Kingdom false because some of the people in it still stink. Do not let somebody else's animal manifestation become your excuse to stop eating spiritual food. Do not become an animal because somebody else acted like one. The devils sit back laughing when church people do their work for them. They love it when one person's untransformed reaction pushes ten others out of alignment.

The Kingdom of God Must Flow Through Your Soul

This is the line that explains everything.

The Kingdom of God must flow through your soul.

Jesus said, *"He that believeth on me, as the scripture hath said, out of his belly shall flow rivers of living water"* (John 7:38, KJV). The river is real. The Spirit is pure. But the river does not bypass your soul. It must flow through the inward man.

"He that believeth on me, as the scripture hath said, out of his belly shall flow rivers of living water." (John 7:38, KJV)

There is a place near Saint Louis where the Mississippi and Missouri Rivers come together. One stream carries darker soil. The other carries lighter soil. For a long stretch you can see two colors running side by side, visibly blending before they finally become one mighty current. The water is real in both channels, but each stream has been flavored by the ground it passed through.

That is how many believers are.

The river of God is real, but the soul still carries old fear, old pride, old shame, old offense, old religion, old reactions, and old wounds. The Spirit may be present, but what comes through the channel still bears the coloring of what trained the soul before truth renewed it. Whatever is in your soul flavors the river.

A man can grow up in a denomination his whole life and never be truly converted to Christ. A person can learn language, ritual, reflex, vocabulary, and behavior around Christianity without ever being born again. But when that person truly has a born-again experience, the spirit comes alive. The issue then is that the soul may still carry years of old religious training.

So, a man may come out of a Catholic background and be genuinely born again, yet still have a soul trained by incense, ritual, titles, gestures, reflexes, and old associations. He sees a man in priestly clothing and instinctively says, "Hello, Father." Why? Because his spirit may now belong to Christ, but his soul is still answering from old grooves. The river is real, but it is still flowing through a channel full of inherited reflex.

And the same thing can happen with any other background. A man can have a Baptist soul, a Pentecostal soul, a Nazarene soul, a charismatic soul, or a tradition-bound soul of any kind. The denomination is not the point. The point is that the spirit may be born again while the soul still needs restoring. The river is real, but the channel still needs healing.

Another man has a Baptist soul. Tell him to lift his hands, and those hands come up exactly to shoulder height and stop as if there is an invisible ceiling. Why? Because in the world that shaped him, praise had rules, expression had limits, and armpit praise never made the approved list. So the river is there, but the soul keeps censoring the response.

Another walks into a church culture where worship is freer, but the soul still does not know how to respond. He is standing there trying to look engaged, but he is still guarded, still watching, still measuring the room. Somebody next to him jabs him in the ribs and says, "Sing." He says, "I am singing." Then the elbow lands harder, the air shoots out of him, and what comes out is the first real sound he made all night. It was almost involuntary worship. Why? Because the soul had been taught how to observe church before it had been taught how to yield in it.

That is the point.

People keep judging the river without understanding the soul it is flowing through.

If the soul is bitter, the flow gets bitter in expression. If the soul is fearful, the flow gets fearful in expression. If the soul is cluttered, the flow gets muddy in reception. If the soul is proud, the flow gets distorted in tone. If the soul is ashamed, the flow gets constricted in boldness. The river is not the problem. The channel is.

That is also why people mistake soul style for spirituality. One man comes out of a rough background. He wears leather, rides hard, looks rough, carries the marks of a different world, and church people instantly start measuring him by externals. But some of what they are looking at is not demonization. It is soul style. The issue is not whether the soul has style. The issue is whether the soul is being sanctified. Religion always wants to crucify what God sometimes intends to sanctify.

So no, the river is not fake because the channel still has color in it. But the color must be dealt with. The soul must be restored. The soul must be renewed. The soul must be brought into order so what is flowing from God can move through the inward man without mixture, distortion, fear, and mud.

That is also why old conditioning keeps showing up after genuine encounters with God. A man can be truly touched by God and still answer life through old reflexes, old religion, old wounds, and old learned responses until the soul gets renewed. The touch may be real, but the soul still needs restoration. That is why this chapter matters. If the inward man stays mixed, what should flow with life keeps coming out muddy.

The Soul Must Be Restored

God never intended for the inward man to stay fractured.

He does not save your spirit and then act unconcerned about the condition of your soul. He restores the soul. He repairs the inward life. He heals what sin bruised, what fear bent, what religion restricted, and what damage taught to hide.

"He restoreth my soul: he leadeth me in the paths of righteousness for his name's sake." (Psalm 23:3, KJV)

That means understanding your soul damage is not a bad day. It is a hopeful day. It means if your responses are mixed, they can be healed. If your mind is cluttered, it can be renewed. If your will is weak, it can be strengthened. If your emotions are unstable, they can be brought into order. If your old history keeps coloring your present response, God can deal with the coloring in the channel.

The Spirit of God does not bypass your humanity. He brings it under government. He does not baptize confusion and call it maturity. He does not bless mixture and call it individuality. He restores the soul.

Conclusion: What You Refuse to Diagnose, You Cannot Heal

You cannot heal what you refuse to diagnose.

If you keep treating your feelings as your identity, you will never diagnose your soul correctly. If you keep defending what truth exposes, you will stay divided. If you keep calling inward disorder normal, you will keep building life on a damaged foundation.

The battle begins in the unseen man. That is where lies must be confronted, dullness broken, appetite subdued, perception restored, and the soul brought back under the rule of Christ.

You are more than what you feel. You are more than your fear, your sadness, your irritation, your craving, your confusion, your reaction, or your inward weather. Your feelings may report a condition, but they are not qualified to govern your life.

God is.

And when the Word is allowed to divide rightly, when the soul is renewed, and when the inward man is brought back under the government of Christ, restoration begins. Not image. Not performance. Not polished religion. Wholeness.

You do not need a new Jesus. You need the unseen man restored.

"Behold, thou desirest truth in the inward parts..." (Psalm 51:6, KJV)

If you do not diagnose the wound, you will keep medicating symptoms. If you do not diagnose the soul, you will keep blaming scenery for what is broken in the unseen man. But once truth names the real condition, heaven can target the healing.

What truth exposes, God can restore.

Scripture Index:

- Genesis 9:15
- Job 5:7
- Psalm 23:3
- Psalm 51:6
- Proverbs 14:12
- Matthew 4:4
- Matthew 6:11
- John 7:38
- Romans 7:14
- Romans 8:7
- Romans 8:21
- Romans 12:2
- 1 Thessalonians 5:23
- Hebrews 4:12
- James 1:8

Chapter Two

Kill the Beast

Introduction: The Flesh Is Not Neutral

Most people do not mind talking about weakness.

They do not mind talking about struggle.

They do not mind talking about needing grace.

But they do not like talking about the beast.

They do not like being told that part of what keeps resisting God in them is not misunderstood innocence. It is not harmless humanity. It is not just personality. It is not merely how they are wired. There is something in fallen human nature that lunges against the rule of Christ. Something that wants appetite without government, desire without restraint, emotion without truth, and self without a cross.

That is why this chapter has to speak plainly.

The flesh is not neutral.

It is not passive.

It is not harmless.

It does not need a little polish and better manners. It does not drift toward holiness by accident. It does not wake up loving the will of God. Scripture says the carnal mind is enmity against God (Romans 8:7). That is not mild language. That is war language.

"Because the carnal mind is enmity against God: for it is not subject to the law of God, neither indeed can be." (Romans 8:7, KJV)

And if Chapter 1 showed you that you are more than what you feel, Chapter 2 must show you why your feelings cannot be trusted to govern you. Part of what you feel is passing through a fallen nature that still wants its own way. Part of what you feel comes through a body that carries appetite, instinct, impulse, and craving. Part of what you feel rises from a flesh-life that would gladly rule you if you let it.

That is why the war is fierce.

Not because God is cruel.

Because what fights Him in you is real.

This generation has been trained to flatter what should be crucified. It has been taught to protect what should be confronted, rename what should be judged, and express what should be nailed down. It has been told that honesty means total surrender to impulse. It has been told that authenticity means never resisting appetite. It has been told that whatever rises in you deserves to live.

No.

Some things rising in you need to die.

The Animal Nature Must Be Crucified

You are a spirit. You have a soul. You live in a body.

And that body is not a side issue.

It is an animal body.

That offends religious softness and human vanity at the same time, which is one reason the truth is so useful. People dress it up, perfume it up, decorate it, flatter it, present it, and polish it. But under all the presentation, it still carries appetite, instinct, impulse, craving, and reaction. No matter how you style it, you are still dressing an animal.

That is why when people get drunk, lustful, violent, manipulative, or out of control, they start acting like animals. The issue is not that the flesh is uneducated. The issue is that the flesh is uncrucified.

When something rises in you opposite to the nature of Christ, that is not heaven coming out of you. That bitterness was not heaven. That outburst was not heaven. That lust was not heaven. That revenge fantasy was not heaven. That controlling mood was not heaven. That manipulative silence was not heaven.

That was the beast talking.

And your flesh does not care whether you go to heaven or go to hell. Why? Because there is no plan of salvation for your flesh. It does not care. The flesh is not interested in your destiny.

It is interested in gratification. It wants what it wants when it wants it, and it wants your whole life arranged around satisfying it. Scripture says

"Let not sin therefore reign in your mortal body, that ye should obey it in the lusts thereof." (Romans 6:12, KJV)

That is why the body is a servant, not a king. The flesh is a vehicle, not a voice of truth. And the body is part of you, but it is a disastrous ruler. When the body rules, appetite rules. When appetite rules, discernment dies. And, when discernment dies, life gets animal fast.

That is also why anointed people can still act animal. The presence of gifting does not prove the beast is dead. When God anoints you, He is anointing a creature that still has to stay under a cross. Power does not excuse flesh. It exposes whether the soul will stay under rule.

Any voice in you that says it is unreasonable to deny yourself, unreasonable to resist appetite, unreasonable to walk in restraint, unreasonable to obey quickly, is your animal nature or the devil talking to you. Scripture says, "be ye transformed by the renewing of your mind" (Romans 12:2). In the pressure of this message, that means your soul must be transformed and your animal nature must be crucified. God is not trying to help the beast express itself more honestly. He is bringing your inner life under rule.

The Flesh Does Not Want the Rule of Christ

The flesh does not negotiate honestly with God because it does not want the rule of Christ.

By definition, whatever is not for Christ is against Christ.

That is why the flesh is anti-Christ in nature.

It is not the final beast of prophecy, but it is beastly enough to destroy your life if you let it lead you. People spend too much time obsessing over some future dark figure while refusing to deal with the anti-Christ resistance rising in their own flesh right now.

There is no next version of Jesus.

There is no softer Christ.

There is no updated Lord who will agree to coexist peacefully with your beast.

The problem is not that Christ needs revising.

The problem is that people want a Lord who will leave the beast alive.

But Christ did not come to negotiate with the flesh. He came to judge it, expose it, and bring a people under rule. That is why He said deny yourself, take up your cross, and follow Me (Matthew 16:24; Luke 9:23).

"Then said Jesus unto his disciples, If any man will come after me, let him deny himself, and take up his cross, and follow me." (Matthew 16:24, KJV)

"And he said to them all, If any man will come after me, let him deny himself, and take up his cross daily, and follow me." (Luke 9:23, KJV)

Deal with the beast in you.

The flesh is not your ally in discipleship.

It does not wake up agreeing with God.

It wakes up wanting to manifest.

Domesticated Religion Is Not Transformation

Many churches do not kill the beast.

They domesticate it.

They teach it to sit still in service.

They teach it to smile on cue.

They teach it to say "praise the Lord" while still full of pride.

They teach it when to stand, when to clap, when to nod, when to look reverent, and how to survive a service without ever coming under a cross.

But behavior management is not transformation.

Polish is not power.

And a room full of controlled flesh is still a room full of flesh.

That is one of the great deceptions of religion. It can make people look manageable without making them holy. It can train them to act nice for an hour and still leave the beast alive. It can produce a room full of mannered animals.

That is why so many churches feel safe while remaining weak. They do not want sons under government. They want nice people. They want the kind of people who do not rock the boat, do not confront sin, do not cast out devils, do not obey too radically, do not pray too hard, do not repent too deeply, and do not disturb the comfortable mood of the room.

But God is not after an audience.

He is after an army.

Armies are not formed by domesticating the flesh.

Armies are formed by bringing lives under rule.

Behavior can be trained.

Nature must be judged.

Nice People Are Not the Same as Holy People

Nice is not holy.

Nice can smile and still be proud.

Nice can serve and still be lustful.

Nice can sound gentle and still be bitter.

Nice people can sound holy in public. They can say amen and hallelujah with the right tone, the right timing, and the right church face, while inside they are polluted. Their mouth says one thing in public, then lies, gossips, and tears apart pastors, ministers, leaders, and other people out of the brokenness of their own soul.

Nice can be politically careful and still be inwardly feral.

That is why niceness is such a dangerous substitute.

It makes people feel safe while leaving them unchanged.

Scripture warns of people who have *"a form of godliness, but denying the power thereof"* (2 Timothy 3:5, KJV).

A form can remain after power is gone.

A reputation can remain after truth is resisted.

A polished exterior can remain while the inward man stays unsubdued.

Holiness is different.

Holiness confronts what niceness covers.

Holiness exposes what niceness manages.

Holiness kills what niceness trains.

Holiness is not interested in helping the flesh look harmless.

Holiness is interested in bringing life under government.

So when people say, "But they are such nice people," that is not the final test. Nice people can still be full of compromise, full of gossip, full of lust, full of passivity, full of fear, full of religious vanity, and full of subtle rebellion. Nice does not prove crucifixion. Nice often only proves social training.

Everything is not fine.

A well-mannered beast is still a beast.

Why Untouched Flesh Keeps Producing Chaos

Every living thing must be fed.

Dead men do not eat.

That line is not only about spirit-life. It exposes why untouched flesh keeps taking over. If a person will not feed the inward man, then the body and its appetites will start occupying more and more territory. When people say they are Christians but never open the Word, never cultivate real prayer, never build private discipline, never seek God intentionally, and never submit to truth deeply, it does not mean nothing is happening.

Something is happening.

Their animal nature is gaining ground.

It often means they are undernourished Christians.

Their spirit is not being fed.

Their soul is not being transformed.

And their animal nature is taking over.

That is why the flesh keeps producing chaos. It has not been denied. It has not been weakened. It has not been brought under rule. It is simply being allowed to live loudly. A man who keeps feeding appetite while starving spirit should not be shocked when appetite starts ruling. A woman who keeps feeding emotion while starving truth should not be shocked when emotion becomes unstable and manipulative.

They are functioning as underfed men.

And underfed men are unstable men.

The cross is not for your boss.

The cross is not for your spouse.

The cross is not for your pastor.

The cross is not for fixing other people first.

It is for killing what keeps fighting God in you. Scripture says to *"walk in the Spirit, and ye shall not fulfil the lust of the flesh,"* because *"the flesh lusteth against the Spirit, and the Spirit against the flesh"* (Galatians 5:16–17, KJV). This is not a small irritation. It is active conflict.

The Cross Was Given to Kill What Keeps Fighting God

Scripture does not tell you to improve the beast.

It tells you what to do with it.

"And they that are Christ's have crucified the flesh with the affections and lusts." (Galatians 5:24, KJV)

Not improved it.

Not renamed it.

Not excused it.

Not made peace with it.

Not taught it how to sit quietly in church.

Crucified it.

The cross was given to kill it.

That does not mean you hate yourself.

It means you stop protecting what is trying to destroy you.

It means you stop calling carnal impulse "just being real."

It means you stop letting fallen nature dress itself up as identity.

It means you stop defending the very thing that keeps fighting heaven in you.

Some things in you need healing.

Some things in you need restoring.

And some things in you need crucifixion.

That is why Jesus said take up your cross daily (Luke 9:23).

Daily.

Because the flesh keeps trying to live daily.

Scripture says:

"For if ye live after the flesh, ye shall die: but if ye through the Spirit do mortify the deeds of the body, ye shall live." (Romans 8:13, KJV)

Mortify.

Put to death.

Not admire from a safe distance.

Not study as a theory.

Not rename as personality.

Kill.

And again Scripture presses even harder:

"Mortify therefore your members which are upon the earth..." (Colossians 3:5, KJV)

God wants to kill the thing that is killing you.

The altar is where something dies.

Not where you visit emotionally for a few minutes and then carry the same beast back to your seat.

That is part of the weakness of modern altar culture. Too many people come chewing gum, standing politely, having a moment, shedding no real tears, yielding no real death, and taking the same thing home that should have been nailed down. The altar is not where you manage image. It is where something dies.

The thing killing your marriage.

The thing killing your hunger.

The thing killing your health.

The thing killing your peace.

The thing killing your future.

God says, bring it here and let it die.

Grace Does Not Train the Beast to Live

Grace is not permission.

Grace is not God learning to tolerate what He already told you to crucify.

Grace is training.

Grace teaches.

Grace brings salvation, but it also teaches you to deny ungodliness and worldly lusts and to live soberly, righteously, and godly in this present world.

"For the grace of God that bringeth salvation hath appeared to all men, Teaching us that, denying ungodliness and worldly lusts, we should live soberly, righteously, and godly, in this present world;" (Titus 2:11-12, KJV)

So if your definition of grace keeps leaving the beast untouched, your definition is broken.

Grace does not train compromise.

Grace trains denial.

Grace trains sobriety.

Grace trains rule.

That is why Paul could say, *"I keep under my body, and bring it into subjection"* (1 Corinthians 9:27, KJV). He did not let giftedness excuse undisciplined flesh. He brought his body under rule.

That verse belongs in this chapter because it makes the point plain: even anointed men must bring the body under government.

Fleshly Lusts Are Warring Against the Soul

This war is not theoretical.

It is not poetic only.

It is not symbolic only.

The flesh wars against the soul.

That is why Scripture says, *"Dearly beloved, I beseech you as strangers and pilgrims, abstain from fleshly lusts, which war against the soul"* (1 Peter 2:11, KJV).

That means fleshly indulgence is not just a moral problem. It is a soul problem. It clouds discernment, weakens will, disorders emotion, stains memory, distorts attachment, and pollutes perception. That is why the beast is never harmless. It is always taking territory somewhere.

If it is not judged, it will make the soul weaker.

If it is not crucified, it will make the soul dirtier.

If it is not denied, it will keep fighting what God is trying to build in you.

Conclusion: What You Refuse to Crucify Will Keep Ruling You

The war is simple, even when it is fierce.

Kill the beast.

Not pet it.

Not flatter it.

Not rename it.

Not hide it under church language.

Not manage it with niceness.

Kill it.

If you keep sparing what God told you to crucify, it will keep speaking in your reactions, your appetites, your moods, your habits, your relationships, and your private contradictions. What you refuse to crucify will keep ruling you.

But if you bring it to the cross, it can lose its right to rule.

This is where clarity begins.

This is where government begins.

This is where freedom begins.

This is where the soul starts coming back under Christ instead of appetite.

The beast does not need better manners.

It needs a cross.

What you refuse to crucify will keep ruling you.

And what you keep nailing to the cross will keep losing power.

Scripture Index:

- Matthew 16:24
- Luke 9:23
- Romans 6:12
- Romans 8:7
- Romans 8:13
- Romans 12:2
- 1 Corinthians 9:27
- Galatians 5:16-17
- Galatians 5:24
- Colossians 3:5
- 1 Thessalonians 5:23
- 2 Timothy 3:5
- Titus 2:11-12
- 1 Peter 2:11

Chapter Three

The Mystery is in Your Sin History

Introduction: Damage Has a Doorway

Everybody has soul damage.

That is not condemnation.

That is diagnosis.

Everybody who comes into the Kingdom has to deal with the animal nature and the soul damage left behind by sin. Some were damaged by what they did. Some were damaged by what was done to them. Some were bruised by lust, rebellion, addiction, secrecy, fear, shame, compromise, and perversion. Others were bent by bad fathers, crooked authority, false religion, manipulators, dictators, gossipers, drunkards, and environments that taught the soul to survive instead of live.

History leaves marks.

Sin leaves residue.

Shame leaves impressions.

That is why the mystery is in your sin history.

Most people know they hurt. Fewer know where the damage entered. Fewer still know how much of what they call personality is really untreated injury. They react and call it discernment. They shut down and call it wisdom. They hide and call it maturity. They go numb and call it peace. But damage does not become harmless because it became familiar.

Damage has a doorway.

If the doorway stays hidden, healing stays random. Then people try to fix precisely what they never identified. They throw verses at wounds they never diagnosed. They apply pressure where truth was needed. They prescribe remedies without understanding the injury. What should have become restoration turns into management.

The soul remembers what trained it.

That is why a man can get genuinely saved and still have an old soul response. He may love Jesus now, but his soul still reacts from old fear, old religion, old shame, old culture, old family patterns, and old learned behaviors. That does not mean the new birth was fake. It means the history still has to be brought under truth.

Sin Always Leaves a Mark on the Soul

Sin is never just an act.

It is an impact.

Whenever you commit a sin, there are side effects of that sin. Those side effects do damage to the mind, the will, the emotions, the memories, the imagination, the personality, and the inward life. The event may be over, but the effect keeps speaking. The act may be forgiven, but the damage still has to be healed.

How Soul Damage Forms

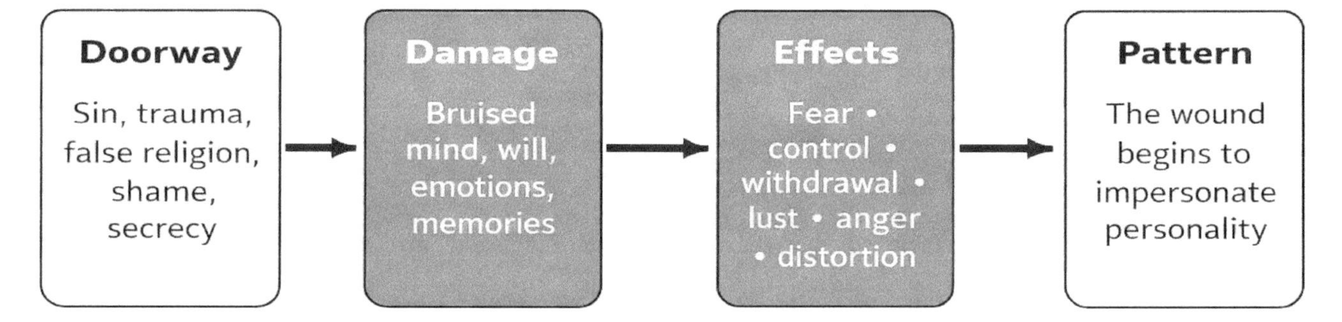

Ps. 23:3 • Rom. 6:23

That is why people can be genuinely saved and still be badly bruised in the soul.

"He restoreth my soul: he leadeth me in the paths of righteousness for his name's sake." (Psalm 23:3, KJV)

If the soul needs restoring, then the soul can be damaged. If the Shepherd restores, then the damage is real. This is not poetic softness. This is not sentimental religion. This is God telling you plainly that salvation and soul restoration are not the same conversation.

You can be forgiven and still need healing.

You can love God and still have damaged reactions.

You can be born again and still need your soul restored.

The act was the doorway.

The damage was the aftermath.

And if the damage is never named, it keeps writing itself into how you think, feel, trust, respond, and live.

This is also why not all damage comes only from obvious evil. Some damage comes from false religion, controlling systems, bad teaching, and years of learning wrong responses. Scripture distinguishes spirit, soul, and body (1 Thessalonians 5:23), and that matters here. A man may be genuinely touched by God and still carry a fearful soul, a suspicious soul, a performance soul, a shut-down soul, or a religion-trained soul.

The river may be real, but it still has to pass through whatever the soul has become.

Think of where two rivers merge but still carry different color for miles. The water is real in both channels, but each stream still bears the memory of the soil it flowed through.

That is how many believers are. The river of God is real, but the soul still carries the coloring of old shame, old fear, old pride, old wounds, old religion, and old learned reactions. The Spirit may be present, but what flows out still bears residue.

Same river, different souls.

The Side Effects of Sin Are Never Small

Sin never arrives empty-handed.

It always carries side effects.

People want forgiveness without fallout. They want mercy without consequence. They want the blood of Jesus treated like a divine eraser while they ignore what the event did to the soul. But sin does not merely need pardoning. Sin leaves damage that needs restoring.

It works like those pharmaceutical commercials. The opening scene is beautiful. Everybody is smiling. Everything looks clean, free, painless. Then the fast voice starts listing what else may happen. You wanted relief from one problem. Now you have ten more you never planned to carry. Now the side effects start rolling: diarrhea or constipation (really, you could not engineer one or the other? It has to be random?) suicidal thoughts, bad breath, mental torment, instability, and leaky bowel syndrome (really?) and all kinds of misery you did not sign up for. You took one thing hoping for relief and picked up a whole train of consequences behind it.

That is how sin works.

It advertises pleasure and hides the wreckage in the fast voice.

It promises pleasure, then leaves distortion.

It promises secrecy, then leaves shame.

It promises relief, then leaves torment.

It promises control, then leaves fracture.

It offers one moment and then invoices the soul for years.

"For the wages of sin is death; but the gift of God is eternal life through Jesus Christ our Lord." (Romans 6:23, KJV)

Death does not wait for the grave to start working. It begins eroding the inward man now. It poisons trust. It disorders desire. It bruises memory. It bends perception. It trains the soul to answer life from damage instead of truth.

That is why repentance is not the end of the matter. Repentance changes direction. Restoration heals damage. Both matter.

This is also why bitterness, suspicion, lust, fear, rage, and inward collapse cannot always be treated like isolated moods. Many times they are the side effects of a deeper doorway. The event happened once, but the consequence kept teaching the soul afterward.

"Looking diligently lest any man fail of the grace of God; lest any root of bitterness springing up trouble you, and thereby many be defiled;" (Hebrews 12:15, KJV)

Roots do not shout first.

They hide first.

Then they trouble later.

The side effects of sin are never small.

Hidden Wounds Keep Speaking

Hidden wounds do not stay hidden in effect. They stay hidden only in explanation.

They keep talking through anger, defensiveness, sarcasm, lust, withdrawal, suspicion, fear, control, and inward collapse. A hidden wound will answer before your mouth does. It will speak through tone. It will speak through timing. It will speak through relationships. It will turn ordinary moments into battles because the wound is still alive enough to be touched.

"And they heard the voice of the LORD God walking in the garden in the cool of the day... And Adam and his wife hid themselves from the

That pattern did not die in Eden. Unresolved issues still drive the soul into hiding. But even where hiding is present, the larger issue is still this: if the wound is not identified, the aftermath keeps ruling.

Many times people are not meeting the real you.

They are interacting with your soul damage.

They are interacting with a wound.

They are interacting with a reaction.

They are interacting with a version of you shaped by injury, fear, rejection, control, shame, false teaching, or suppression.

If it still speaks, it still rules somewhere.

"He that covereth his sins shall not prosper: but whoso confesseth and forsaketh them shall have mercy." (Proverbs 28:13, KJV)

Mercy reaches what hiding kept sealed.

Specific Damage Requires Specific Healing

If you do not know what was damaged, how it was damaged, what entered, what hardened, what lied to you, what shut you down, what deformed your responses, and what trained the soul to act this way, then healing stays broad and vague.

That is why the mystery is in the history.

When you know the history, you know where to target healing. But if you hide the history, you cover up the mystery, and now everybody is trying to fix you in the dark.

It is like walking into a pharmacy with money in your hand and saying, "I feel bad. Sell me five hundred dollars' worth of medicine. We will just try things at random."

So they start pulling everything off the shelf. Something for nerves. Something for pain. Something for infection. Something for sleep. Something for inflammation.

That is how damaged souls often get handled.

Random advice.

Random rebukes.

Random altar calls.

Random correction.

Random pressure.

Random principles.

Everybody doing something.

Nobody touching the wound.

But if the damage is specifically identified, healing stops being vague. Now the right scriptures can be applied. Now the right counsel can be given. Now the right place can be opened. Now the Shepherd can touch the actual bruise instead of everybody guessing at symptoms.

"Confess your faults one to another, and pray one for another, that ye may be healed." (James 5:16, KJV)

Healing is tied to truth.

Not performance.

Not spectacle.

Not random activity.

Truth.

Time Does Not Heal What Truth Has Not Touched

Time can age a wound without curing it. Time can bury pain without healing it. Time can make you quieter without making you whole. If something from twenty years ago can still make you rage, panic, recoil, go numb, shut down, or spiral, then time did not heal it. Time merely carried it.

That is why people can be years removed from an event and still react like it happened yesterday. One name, one reminder, one tone, one familiar pressure, or one passing resemblance can still ignite the whole inward man. Time did not heal it. The wound was carried forward untreated.

And when the soul stays unbalanced, the problem is not that you become less saved. The problem is that the life of God cannot pass through your soul cleanly. Unrestored places become narrow places. Damaged places become restricted places. What should have flowed through you gets pinched by what still has not healed.

"Beloved, I wish above all things that thou mayest prosper and be in health, even as thy soul prospereth." (3 John 1:2, KJV)

Soul condition matters.

"And be renewed in the spirit of your mind;" (Ephesians 4:23, KJV)

God does not merely want you older.

He wants you renewed.

Scar Tissue and Open Wounds Are Not the Same

There is a difference between scar tissue and an infected wound.

A scar means something happened.

An infected wound means something is still happening.

A scar can be slapped, pressed, or pinched without pain because it has healed. But an infected wound barely gets brushed and the whole system reacts. That is how the soul works too. If the past is mentioned and you instantly swell with rage, fear, shame, nausea, defensiveness, or collapse, that is not just memory. That is evidence that the wound is still alive.

When the soul is bruised, ordinary touch can feel like threat. Ordinary correction can feel unbearable. Ordinary love can feel invasive. That is not because normal became evil. It is because damage made normal contact feel dangerous.

If you cannot talk about the past without getting pulled under by it, you cannot use it as testimony yet.

Some people want the dignity of scar tissue while still carrying an infected wound. But heaven is not confused.

A scar can testify.

An infected wound can only react.

"Then saith he to Thomas, Reach hither thy finger, and behold my hands..." (John 20:27, KJV)

God does not pretend history never happened. He heals it so thoroughly that what once bled can now witness. The handling of your scar becomes somebody else's testimony of the glory of God.

Conclusion: The Place of Damage Is the Place God Targets for Restoration

The place of damage is not the place God avoids.

It is the place He targets.

"The Spirit of the Lord is upon me, because he hath anointed me to preach the gospel to the poor; he hath sent me to heal the brokenhearted, to preach deliverance to the captives, and recovering of sight to the blind, to set at liberty them that are bruised." (Luke 4:18, KJV)

That is targeted restoration.

Brokenhearted.

Captive.

Blind.

Bruised.

God wants to restore the soul. That means understanding your soul damage is not a bad day. It is an excellent day for restoration. If you were the child of divorce, there can be restoration. If you did drugs, there can be restoration. If you lived in fornication, fear, secrecy, shame, rebellion, or inner fragmentation, there can be restoration. If false religion, manipulative voices, or years of survival thinking bent your soul out of shape, there can be restoration.

The name of the sin points to the doorway.

The consequences point to the damage.

And God targets what sin damaged.

So stop protecting what God is trying to heal.

Stop polishing what God is trying to expose.

Stop calling untreated damage maturity because enough years have passed.

Stop asking for random medicine when the Holy Spirit is ready to bring targeted restoration.

The mystery is in your sin history.

When the history comes into the light, healing stops being random.

When the wound is named, the Shepherd can touch it.

When the damage is no longer concealed, restoration stops being vague.

What sin marked, Christ can restore.

What shame bruised, Christ can heal.

What was hidden can come under light.

And what comes under light can come under the hand of God.

Scripture Index:

- Genesis 3:8-10
- Psalm 23:3
- Proverbs 28:13
- Luke 4:18
- John 20:27
- Romans 6:23
- 1 Thessalonians 5:23
- Hebrews 12:15
- James 5:16
- 3 John 1:2
- Ephesians 4:23

Part II

How Hell Fractures the Soul

Hell does not merely tempt. It stains. It conceals. It dulls. It fractures. Once the doorway of damage is exposed, the next burden is light. These chapters move into edited truth, hidden wounds, dehumanization, desensitization, and the way darkness trains a soul until wrong starts feeling normal. This section is not soft because concealment is not soft. It breaks the alliance between secrecy and survival. It drags what has been managed into the open, strips cover from protected bondage, and makes the reader face the place where darkness has been feeding on the inward man. What stays hidden stays untreated. What comes into the light can come under the hand of God.

"But he that doeth truth cometh to the light, that his deeds may be made manifest, that they are wrought in God." (John 3:21, KJV)

Chapter Four

He Cannot restore What you Won't Reveal

Introduction: Heaven Works in the Light

God does not restore the hidden man by cooperating with darkness.

He does not heal through edited truth, polished language, selective confession, and religious concealment. He works in light. He works where the soul opens. He works where the lie loses cover and the wound is no longer protected. That is the dividing line many people keep resisting. They want relief, but they do not want unveiling. They want peace, but they do not want exposure. They want God to heal what they are still protecting from His hand.

But heaven does not pour remedy into a sealed place.

There is no place to put the remedy until the soul opens.

That is why truth is not optional in restoration. God is not interested in treating your public version while your inward life stays barricaded. He is not healing the managed self. He is after the real man, the real woman, the actual place where damage entered, where fear settled, where shame learned to hide, where the soul became restricted by its own affections.

"O ye Corinthians, our mouth is open unto you, our heart is enlarged. Ye are not straitened in us, but ye are straitened in your own bowels." (2 Corinthians 6:11-12, KJV)

What stays hidden stays untreated.

What stays concealed stays unhealed.

And what comes into the light can finally come under the hand of God.

Concealment Protects Bondage, Not Healing

Concealment has never protected healing.

It has only protected bondage.

People hide because hiding feels safer than honesty. They hide because image feels easier than exposure. They hide because shame teaches the soul to survive by editing. But concealment is not wisdom. It is fear with a religious vocabulary. It is shame trying to keep control. It is darkness defending its address.

"He that covereth his sins shall not prosper: but whoso confesseth and forsaketh them shall have mercy." (Proverbs 28:13, KJV)

Mercy does not meet you where you are pretending.

Mercy meets you where you finally tell the truth.

That is why concealment is so deadly. It allows people to remain impressive while staying infected. It lets them sound mature while inwardly remaining bound. It permits them to keep the language of healing while refusing the doorway healing requires. They say enough to look honest, but not enough to get free. They admit distress, but not disobedience. They confess pain, but not the idol. They mention the symptom, but not the doorway. They tell enough truth to manage perception while hiding enough truth to preserve bondage.

That is not healing.

That is damage under cover.

The Soul Hides Before the Mouth Lies

The mouth is not where hiding begins.

The soul hides first.

Adam did not start with explanation. He started with hiding. That is still the reflex of damaged people. The soul ducks light before the lips ever form a sentence. It hides in silence, in vagueness, in over-control, in false calm, in polished church language, in selective memory, in distance, in avoidance, in jokes, in defensiveness, and in that learned habit of always staying just beyond reach.

"And they heard the voice of the LORD God walking in the garden in the cool of the day... and Adam and his wife hid themselves... And he said, I heard thy voice in the garden, and I was afraid... and I hid myself." (Genesis 3:8-10, KJV)

Some people are not difficult to heal because God is unwilling.

They are difficult to heal because they are difficult to locate.

They have lived edited for so long that even they no longer know where the real wound begins. They can testify without touching the truth. They can speak clean sentences while the inward man remains sealed. They can say, "I'm fine," while their reactions keep proving the soul is still bruised. They can look composed while something inside them is still bleeding.

That is what hidden damage does. It makes the false version easier to access than the real one.

And if nobody can get to the real thing, there is no place to put the remedy.

Partial Truth Is Still Darkness

Partial truth does not become light because it contains facts.

A partial truth is a whole lie.

If it is being used to protect darkness, it is still darkness.

That is why edited confession is so dangerous. It gives enough detail to sound open while withholding enough detail to stay in control. It reveals the injury but protects the rebellion. It admits the collapse but conceals the compromise. It names the wound but not the infection. It tells what happened without telling how the soul agreed with lies afterward. It wants sympathy without surrender.

That is still darkness.

"For every one that doeth evil hateth the light, neither cometh to the light, lest his deeds should be reproved." (John 3:20, KJV)

Light is not the enemy of your soul.

Light is the enemy of what has been feeding on your soul.

If you say half of what is true because you are trying to protect the other half, you are not walking in the light. If you disclose enough to calm suspicion but not enough to be healed, you are not in the light. If you want comfort without exposure, you are still negotiating with darkness.

Some people have built whole identities out of edited truth. A version for church. A version for leadership. A version for marriage. A version for themselves. But God does not heal versions. He heals what is naked and open before Him.

"Neither is there any creature that is not manifest in his sight: but all things are naked and opened unto the eyes of him with whom we have to do." (Hebrews 4:13, KJV)

The Word of God does not flatter your cover.

It strips it.

That is why partial disclosure is such a serious thing even in the natural world. If you sell a house and do not disclose what you know is wrong with it, that is not wisdom. That is deception. If you sell a business and hide material facts that another person needed to know, that is not just a technical oversight. That is a lie through omission. In the natural realm, partial disclosure can get you sued because the law understands what many religious people still try to dodge: a partial truth is a whole lie.

And the same thing happens in people-work. Suppose you are hiring for a job and you ask church leadership about a person they are recommending. You ask about the background because people will be affected by the hire. But they recommend the person and do not give full disclosure. They leave out the instability. They leave out the pattern. They leave out the history that matters. That is not honesty. That is not kindness. That is not protecting the church. That is a whole lie through omission. Then the wrong person gets placed in the wrong job, people get harmed, trust gets damaged, and everybody acts surprised as if silence was innocence. It was not innocence. It was concealment dressed up as diplomacy.

"He that is faithful in that which is least is faithful also in much: and he that is unjust in the least is unjust also in much." (Luke 16:10, KJV)

If a person will edit truth when the stakes seem small, do not pretend they are walking in light when the stakes get large.

"Lying lips are abomination to the LORD: but they that deal truly are his delight." (Proverbs 12:22, KJV)

God does not grade lies only by volume. He also judges lies by concealment.

Concealment vs. Restoration

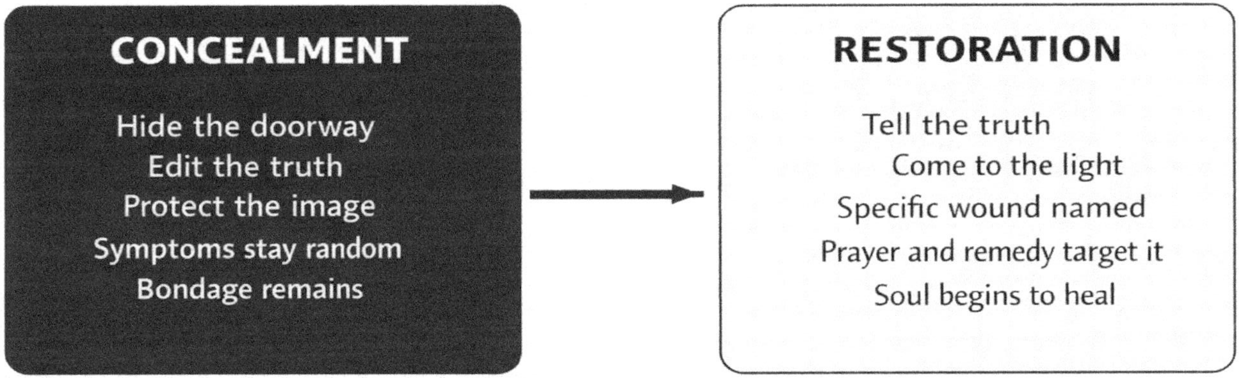

Prov. 28:13 • James 5:16 • John 3:20–21

Confession Opens the Door to Restoration

Confession is not humiliation.

It is access.

It is the locked room opening. It is the sealed place losing its lid. It is the soul stopping its lifelong effort to survive by concealment. Confession does not create damage. It exposes where damage has been ruling untreated.

"Confess your faults one to another, and pray one for another, that ye may be healed."

(James 5:16, KJV)

Healing is tied to truth.

Not performance.

Not spectacle.

Truth.

If the soul stays shut, ministry becomes guesswork. Prayer becomes general. Counsel stays random. Scripture gets applied broadly but not accurately. Everybody keeps throwing help at symptoms while the wound remains unnamed. It is like walking into a pharmacy and saying, "Sell me five hundred dollars' worth of medicine. We will just try things at random."

Unfortunately, this is how many churches operate. They keep handing out random medicine because they do not spend enough time getting to know the people personally. They want to treat crowds without touching wounds. They want to manage symptoms without learning histories. And some leaders act as if personal nearness is dangerous, as if familiarity itself is some kind of unpardonable sin, because they are afraid that if people get close enough to see them as human, the gifts, signs, miracles, and respect will somehow stop working. But that is not Kingdom thinking. That is insecurity dressed up as spirituality.

That is why so much of what comes out of that kind of ministry is random junk wearing church language.

Random advice.

Random rebukes.

Random altar calls.

Random pressure.

Random principles.

Everybody doing something.

Nobody reaching the wound.

But once truth comes forward, restoration stops being random. The Shepherd can touch the exact place. The Spirit can address the actual damage. Light can invade what secrecy protected. That is why confession is mercy. It tells heaven, "You may touch this now."

"If we confess our sins, he is faithful and just to forgive us our sins, and to cleanse us from all unrighteousness." (1 John 1:9, KJV)

Notice the order. Confession is not earning mercy. Confession is opening to mercy.

Shame Cycle

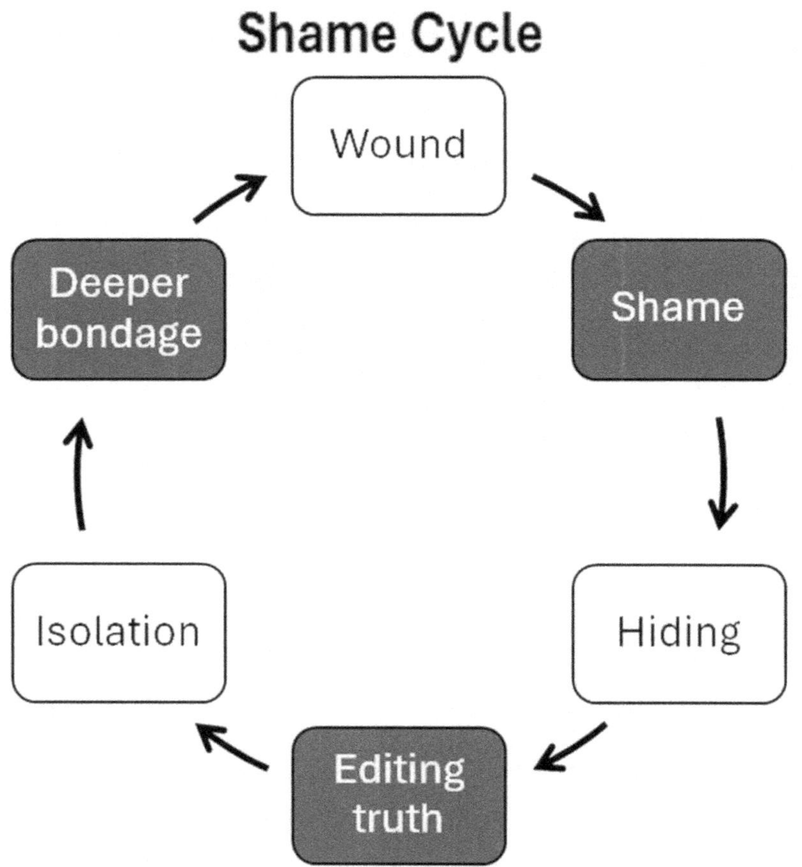

What Shame hides, it keeps feeding.

THE CYCLE BREAKS WHEN TRUTH IS TOLD,
THE SOUL COMES INTO THE LIGHT,
AND THE WOUND IS SPECIFICALLY
BROUGHT TO GOD

PROVERBS 28:13
JOHN 3:20-21
JAMES 5:16

There Is No Place to Put the Remedy

This is one of the clearest pictures in the whole message.

A person was dying in a hospital. The nurse was trying to start an IV, but the veins had collapsed. She kept tapping the arm and working the skin, trying to get a vein to rise. And I asked why she was doing that. The explanation was simple: if the vein does not rise, there is no place to put the remedy.

That is the problem with a sealed soul.

If nothing opens, where will the remedy land?

If the soul stays collapsed, where will healing enter?

If the inward man stays barricaded, where will the medicine go?

There is no place to put the remedy until the soul opens.

Jesus did not stay sealed off from people to protect His image. He moved straight into the crowds because He wanted access to people, and He wanted people to have access to Him.

"But when he saw the multitudes, he was moved with compassion on them..." (Matthew 9:36, KJV)

"And Jesus, when he came out, saw much people, and was moved with compassion toward them... and he began to teach them many things." (Mark 6:34, KJV)

He did not fear closeness. He used closeness. He did not fear knowing people. He healed, taught, corrected, fed, delivered, and restored because He stepped toward them, not away from them.

"I am the good shepherd, and know my sheep, and am known of mine." (John 10:14, KJV)

That is real shepherding.

Then you have the other kind of leader: the Pharisaical kind. They do not want sons and daughters raised up in the Kingdom. They want dependents, admirers, and controlled people orbiting their position.

"Woe unto you, scribes and Pharisees, hypocrites! for ye compass sea and land to make one proselyte, and when he is made, ye make him twofold more the child of hell than yourselves." (Matthew 23:15, KJV)

That is terrifying. It means leadership can become so corrupt that instead of forming people into healthy sons and daughters, it reproduces bondage, pride, blindness, and hellish religion. That is insanity. And every leader who builds that way will answer for it before God.

That is why John the Baptist had to come first. He was preparing the way. He was getting the people open. He was breaking ground so truth could enter. Heaven does not merely want a sermon heard. Heaven wants an opening made.

Sometimes what people need is not a softer word.

Sometimes they need a Holy Ghost can opener.

Sometimes they need the chainsaw of the Spirit cutting through layers of false calm, buried shame, managed appearance, and religious editing until the hidden place finally gives way and opens to light.

That is mercy.

Not because God enjoys cutting.

Because God intends to heal.

Why Specific Healing Requires Specific Honesty

Generic pain rarely receives specific healing.

If you do not know what was damaged, how it was damaged, what entered, what hardened, what lied to you, what shut you down, what you covered, what you normalized, and where the soul stopped responding normally and began reacting from bruising, then healing stays broad and vague. You may feel helped for a moment, but the roots remain untouched.

That is why specific honesty matters.

Not theatrical honesty.

Specific honesty.

A bruised place reacts to ordinary touch. A healed scar does not. That is how soul damage works. A person can be lightly corrected and erupt. They can be ordinarily questioned and shut down. They can be gently approached and instantly withdraw. Why? Because the bruise is still there.

That is why God is not satisfied with edited relief. He wants actual restoration. He wants the soul to stop reacting from buried injury and start responding from truth.

"Create in me a clean heart, O God; and renew a right spirit within me." (Psalm 51:10, KJV)

A right spirit cannot be built on managed dishonesty.

It grows where truth is welcomed all the way down.

"Behold, thou desirest truth in the inward parts: and in the hidden part thou shalt make me to know wisdom." (Psalm 51:6, KJV)

God wants truth in the inward parts, not only in the public presentation.

God Does Not Expose to Shame; He Exposes to Heal

Many people still resist the light because they think exposure means rejection.

It does not.

God does not expose to shame.

He exposes to heal.

He is not uncovering you to mock you. He is not revealing damage to embarrass you. He is not bringing hidden things forward so you can die under them. He is bringing them forward so they stop ruling in secret. He is putting light on what darkness has been feeding on. He is uncovering the wound because He intends to restore the soul.

"For God sent not his Son into the world to condemn the world; but that the world through him might be saved." (John 3:17, KJV)

That is mercy.

Mercy does not leave the infection buried.

Mercy opens it.

Mercy drains it.

Mercy refuses to let secrecy keep poisoning identity.

Some people have confused concealment with dignity. It is not dignity. It is bondage management. Some have confused silence with healing. It is not healing. It is often only compression. Some have confused being quieter with being whole. But time can age a wound without curing it. Religion can polish damage without restoring it. A person can become more presentable while the inward man remains restricted.

God wants more than presentation.

He wants the soul back.

He wants the real man out of hiding.

He wants what has been dehumanized, restricted, bruised, and edited brought back into light, into truth, into feeling, into sanity, into alignment, and into His restoring hand.

Conclusion: What Comes Into the Light Can Come Under the Hand of God

God does not restore what you insist on covering.

He restores what you bring into the light.

Not desire alone.

Not gifting alone.

Not attendance alone.

Not emotional moments alone.

Truth.

Exposure.

Honest agreement with God about what is hidden, what is damaged, what is infected, what is false, and what must be healed.

So stop protecting the wound that is protecting the bondage.

Stop calling vagueness wisdom.

Stop calling concealment maturity.

Stop calling edited truth honesty.

Stop asking for remedy while keeping the soul sealed.

What you hide, you hand to darkness.

What you reveal, you place before God.

And what comes under the light can come under the hand of God.

The Shepherd still restores souls. But He restores them where truth is told, where hiding breaks, where the inward man stops negotiating, and where the sealed room is finally opened.

Bring the real thing forward.

Bring the whole thing forward.

Bring the hidden thing forward.

Because there is no place to put the remedy until the soul opens.

"But he that doeth truth cometh to the light, that his deeds may be made manifest, that they are wrought in God." (John 3:21, KJV)

Scripture Index:

- Genesis 3:8-10
- Psalm 51:6

- Psalm 51:10
- Proverbs 12:22
- Proverbs 28:13
- Matthew 9:36
- Matthew 23:15
- Luke 16:10
- John 3:17
- John 3:20-21
- John 10:14
- Mark 6:34
- 1 John 1:9
- 2 Corinthians 6:11-12
- Hebrews 4:13
- James 5:16

Chapter Five

Dehumanized and Desensitized

Introduction: When the Soul Stops Responding

You have to recognize the society you live in, because whether you meant to be shaped by it or not, you have been living inside it.

You hear it in the ads. You see it on the screens. You feel it in the public tone, the public language, the public madness, the public confusion. You move through a civilization being trained away from God, away from sanity, away from reverence, away from what is clean, and away from what is normal in the Kingdom. And if you keep living inside a desensitized world without discernment, your own soul can start going dull while you still think you are fine.

That is part of the terror of soul damage.

It does not only wound the inward man. It alters what the inward man can still feel. The soul stops responding the way it should. What should disturb you no longer disturbs you. What should awaken grief no longer awakens grief. What should pierce you bounces off. What should make you tremble begins to feel ordinary. Once that happens, the issue is no longer merely the darkness around you. The issue is what that darkness has already done within you.

A damaged soul can call numbness peace.

It can call deadness maturity.

It can call dullness stability.

But when the soul stops responding correctly, something has gone wrong deeper than emotion. Something has gone wrong in perception.

Satan's Strategy Is to Dehumanize

The devil has a plan to destroy people.

He has a plan to destroy families.

He has a plan to destroy societies.

He has a plan to destroy churches.

He has a plan to destroy pastors.

He has a plan to destroy relationships inside churches.

He has a plan to fracture trust, poison covenant, corrupt speech, spread suspicion, and turn wounded people into carriers of more damage.

And some of that damage does not stay in the category of "bad attitude" or "church drama." Some of it crosses into conduct that has kingdom consequences. Pride blinds people to the seriousness of what they are doing. They think they are only exposing somebody else, only cutting somebody else down, only damaging somebody else's name, only injuring a pastor, a minister, a leader, or another believer. But some of those actions do not merely stain relationships. They endanger souls.

A person can get so proud, so bitter, so divisive, so false, so corrupt in speech, and so blind in heart that they stop treating these things like sin at all. They call it discernment. They call it concern. They call it honesty. They call it defending truth. But if what they are actually practicing is slander, hatred, sowing discord, railing accusation, malicious speech, envy, faction, unforgiveness, hypocrisy, or ongoing unrighteousness, Scripture does not treat that lightly. Scripture warns that those who practice such things shall not inherit the kingdom of God (Galatians 5:19-21; 1 Corinthians 6:9-10). If a person does not inherit the kingdom, then where do they go? That is why this is not small. This is not casual. This is not harmless. Pride can make a person think they are damaging somebody else while they are actually gambling with their own eternity.

That is how hell works.

It strips tenderness.

It strips sobriety.

It strips moral reflex.

It strips clean perception.

It strips holy sensitivity.

It drives the inward man downward until the person can still function outwardly while no longer answering heaven normally. A person may keep moving, keep speaking, keep attending, keep working, keep posting, keep buying, keep laughing, keep performing, and still be inwardly lowered.

That is what dehumanization does.

It does not always announce itself with collapse.

Sometimes it appears as adaptation.

Sometimes it appears as modern life.

Sometimes it appears as ordinary people who can no longer feel rightly, receive rightly, or discern rightly because the soul has been repeatedly handled by darkness until it lost its proper reactions.

And once the soul is dehumanized, desensitization is not far behind.

Desensitization Is Not Strength

Some people think they are strong because nothing moves them anymore.

Nothing convicts them deeply. Nothing startles them deeply. Nothing pierces them deeply. They can hear warnings without trembling, hear truth without yielding, hear correction without receiving, and watch darkness spread without grief. They call that balance. They call that maturity. They call that being unbothered.

It is not maturity.

It is injury left untreated long enough to impersonate personality.

A numb soul is not a strong soul.

A shut-down soul is not a healed soul.

Dehumanized → Desensitized → Distorted

When wrong starts feeling normal, the soul has already been wounded.

Matt. 4:16 • Heb. 5:11–14

A desensitized soul is not a stable soul.

If truth no longer moves you, something is wrong. If you can live in contradiction and feel no inward alarm, something is wrong. If holiness feels extreme and compromise feels normal, something is wrong. If everything of God feels distant while everything carnal feels familiar, something is wrong.

"Of whom we have many things to say, and hard to be uttered, seeing ye are dull of hearing." (Hebrews 5:11, KJV)

"For this people's heart is waxed gross, and their ears are dull of hearing, and their eyes they have closed..." (Matthew 13:15, KJV)

"Make the heart of this people fat, and make their ears heavy, and shut their eyes..." (Isaiah 6:10, KJV)

When you no longer feel concern or worry over the sin you are doing, that is a seared conscience. Scripture speaks of people *"having their conscience seared with a hot iron"* (1 Timothy 4:2, KJV). A sear in the flesh is like a hot poker left on too long. At first there is pain because the nerves still work. But if that burning continues long enough, the nerve endings die, and now you do not feel the hot poker the way you once did. After enough time, you will not feel anything at all. The pain is still real. The damage is still real. You just lost the ability to feel it.

That is a very dangerous place to be.

Why? Because your inhibition to that sin is now weakened. The warning system has been damaged. The inward pain that should have told you to stop has gone dull. That does not mean there is no consequence. It means you no longer feel the consequence rightly. And when a person can sin without grief, compromise without trembling, and wound others without inward alarm, that soul is in serious danger.

But if you are recovering and can feel the pain of the sin again, if remorse is returning, if conviction is returning, if you can again feel the weight of what you did, that is not a bad sign. That is mercy. That is evidence that the conscience is waking up. That is evidence that the soul is coming back into feeling. And when that happens, you are on the path to recovery, healing, and deliverance.

"Speaking lies in hypocrisy; having their conscience seared with a hot iron;" (1 Timothy 4:2, KJV)

Dullness of hearing does not mean heaven fell silent.

It means the soul lost its power to answer.

That is the danger.

God can still be speaking while the inward man no longer knows how to respond.

A Dull Soul Can No Longer Receive Correctly

You live your life through your soul.

You receive through your soul. You perceive through your soul. You read relationships through your soul. You hear correction through your soul. You interpret God's dealings through your soul. And when the soul goes dull, life starts going dull with it. Promise feels far away. Healing feels far away. Joy feels far away. Even when truth is present, the person experiences it as distance because the inward instrument of reception has been damaged.

That is why some people keep saying they know the promise is true, but it still feels unreachable.

The distance is not always in God.

Many times the distance is in perception.

A dull soul misreads everything.

It misreads love as control.

It misreads correction as rejection.

It misreads holiness as harshness.

It misreads clarity as attack.

It misreads strong preaching as abuse.

It misreads order because it has lost the ability to recognize Kingdom normal.

"And be not conformed to this world: but be ye transformed by the renewing of your mind..." (Romans 12:2, KJV)

"Having the understanding darkened, being alienated from the life of God through the ignorance that is in them, because of the blindness of their heart: Who being past feeling..." (Ephesians 4:18-19, KJV)

"Because that, when they knew God, they glorified him not as God... but became vain in their imaginations, and their foolish heart was darkened." (Romans 1:21, KJV)

And that is why people can sit near real things and still not receive them. The issue is not always that God is absent. The issue is that the soul has become too dull to receive what is present. The river may be real, but if the soul through which life is being processed is damaged, what should be flowing with clarity gets distorted in reception.

"He that believeth on me, as the scripture hath said, out of his belly shall flow rivers of living water." (John 7:38, KJV)

Some people are not far from truth geographically.

They are far from truth perceptually.

Culture Can Normalize What Heaven Calls Darkness

Culture is not neutral.

It is here to capture you.

And one of the main ways it captures people is by desensitizing them to what is real, what is holy, what is sane, what is clean, and what is normal in the Kingdom of God.

It repeats darkness until darkness feels ordinary.

It stages perversion until perversion feels familiar.

It celebrates confusion until confusion sounds compassionate.

It floods the gates of the soul until repetition removes alarm.

That is how whole populations get trained.

Children grow up inside digital unreality. Families can sit together and barely know how to be present with one another. People lose the capacity for normal relationships while calling it personality, generation, wiring, or preference. Souls get trained by screens, noise, lust, vanity, rage, role confusion, vulgarity, and fantasy until ordinary human presence itself starts becoming difficult.

That is not harmless.

That is formation.

That is a culture teaching souls how not to feel.

And once a society has been conditioned like that, darkness no longer has to hide. It can stand in the open because people have lost the reflex to recoil.

But common is not clean.

Repeated is not righteous.

Popular is not holy.

A society can rehearse bondage so often that it begins calling captivity freedom and confusion authenticity. That is not enlightenment. That is darkness with better marketing.

When Wrong Feels Normal, the Soul Is Already Wounded

Do crazy people know they are crazy?

No.

That is the problem.

You do not know distortion is distortion until it is measured against what is actually normal. And if your measuring rod is a damaged culture, a damaged family line, a damaged church environment, a damaged peer group, or a damaged inner history, then your definition of normal is already corrupt.

That is why wrong can start feeling normal.

The wounded soul adapts.

It adjusts to contradiction.

It adjusts to confusion.

It adjusts to impurity.

It adjusts to broken speech, broken relationships, broken appetites, broken thought patterns, and broken reactions.

Then after enough repetition, the person no longer says, "Something is wrong."

They say, "That is just life."

No.

That is not life.

That is damage.

When wrong feels normal, the soul has already been wounded.

That is why damaged people often defend what is killing them. They are not only in bondage. They are acclimated. The inward alarm system has been weakened. They call compromise wisdom. They call low-level captivity peace. They call numbness balance. They call disordered appetite identity. They call deadened reactions maturity.

"Keep thy heart with all diligence; for out of it are the issues of life." (Proverbs 4:23, KJV)

Sin bondage works like Stockholm syndrome, where a person is captured against their will, abused in captivity, and then starts bonding with the captor. When the captive is freed, the abused starts missing the abuser, defending the abuser, and going back to the very thing that was destroying them, sometimes even searching the captor out again and marrying them. That is what sin does to the soul. Jesus said, *"Whosoever committeth sin is the servant of sin"* (John 8:34, KJV). Peter said, *"Of whom a man is overcome, of the same is he brought in bondage"* (2 Peter 2:19, KJV). The longer sin holds a person, the more warped they become. The more soul-cracked they become. Their loves get bent. Their desires get bent. Their judgment gets bent. Then when freedom comes, part of them still misses the chains because bondage became familiar and freedom feels strange. So they go searching for the captor again. They go back to the poison. They go back to the hand that bruised them. They go back to the thing that degraded them because sin did not just bind their behavior. It trained their soul to long for its own slavery. That is how wicked sin is. It does not only hold you. It teaches you to miss what was killing you.

But Kingdom normal is not measured by what a damaged generation can tolerate.

Kingdom normal is measured by God.

The Church Must Recover Kingdom Normal

The church cannot answer a dehumanized world by becoming softer than heaven.

It cannot answer numbness by entertaining the numb. It cannot answer soul damage by managing symptoms while leaving perception broken. It cannot heal people by lowering the standard until nobody feels disturbed. It cannot redefine dysfunction as personality and then call that mercy.

The answer is not softer darkness.

The answer is Kingdom normal.

Kingdom normal means the soul can respond rightly again.

Kingdom normal means conviction is not treated like cruelty.

Kingdom normal means strong preaching is not treated like violence.

Kingdom normal means ordinary obedience, ordinary tenderness, ordinary truth, ordinary holiness, and ordinary love no longer feel unbearable.

Many people cannot handle normal because the soul has been bruised.

Some cannot handle normal touch.

Some cannot handle normal relationships.

Some cannot handle ordinary faithfulness.

Some cannot enjoy simple obedience.

Some cannot carry ordinary closeness without reacting because unresolved damage has made what is normal feel foreign.

But the answer is not to build doctrine around broken reactions.

The answer is healing.

If you do not care whether people are truly saved, something has gone wrong in the soul. If you can ignore the Holy Spirit in ordinary life without grief, something has gone wrong in the soul. If you can remain unmoved while people stay bound, deceived, numb, and unreached, that is not maturity. That is desensitization.

The church must stop protecting that condition.

It must recover the courage to say that some people are not meeting the real you. They are interacting with your soul damage.

And until that damage is healed, what should flow cleanly through the soul will keep getting restricted, distorted, or shut down.

"O ye Corinthians, our mouth is open unto you, our heart is enlarged. Ye are not straitened in us, but ye are straitened in your own bowels." (2 Corinthians 6:11-12, KJV)

Restricted affections produce restricted lives.

The Restrainer and the Slide Into Madness

There is another reason this subject is so serious.

The Holy Spirit restrains.

When a people keep rejecting truth, mocking restraint, and normalizing lawlessness, they are not just making bad cultural choices. They are weakening the structures that keep insanity from flooding the public square.

"For the mystery of iniquity doth already work: only he who now letteth will let..." (2 Thessalonians 2:7, KJV)

Lawlessness does not merely break rules.

It breaks people.

It releases appetite without government.

It releases desire without boundaries.

It releases human nature without restraint.

That is why societies can get crazier while still calling themselves advanced. If a people lose moral reflex and still congratulate themselves for freedom, they are not moving upward. They are sliding downward while renaming the fall.

The restraining work of the Holy Spirit matters more than many people realize. Without that mercy, darkness does not become more civil. It becomes more obvious.

The Shepherd Restores What Darkness Numbed

This is not hopeless.

It is serious, but it is not hopeless.

What darkness trained, God can undo.

What culture normalized, truth can confront.

What hell numbed, the Holy Ghost can awaken.

That is why Jesus announced not only salvation in general, but targeted restoration for broken human conditions.

"The Spirit of the Lord is upon me, because he hath anointed me to preach the gospel to the poor; he hath sent me to heal the brokenhearted, to preach deliverance to the captives, and recovering of sight to the blind, to set at liberty them that are bruised." (Luke 4:18, KJV)

Brokenhearted.

Captive.

Blind.

Bruised.

Those are not minor words.

Those are soul-condition words.

That means God is not confused about what damage does to people. He knows the inward man can be broken, restricted, blinded, bruised, and held in bondage. And He still announces liberty.

Conclusion: What Hell Numbs, the Holy Ghost Must Awaken

You need to ask the Holy Ghost the hard question.

Have I been dehumanized?

Have I been desensitized?

Has my soul adapted to what I should have resisted?

Has my spirit tolerated what I should have confronted?

Has wrong started feeling normal to me?

Because God wants to bless you, but He has to find an open soul for a remedy.

Not talent.

Not attendance.

Not religious vocabulary.

Not emotional moments.

An open soul.

If the soul does not recognize it has gone dull, where will the remedy land? If the soul refuses to admit it has been dehumanized, where will restoration enter? God is not looking for polished excuses. He is looking for honest agreement. He is looking for the inward man to come back under light and say, "Something is wrong in me, and I will no longer defend it."

"The people which sat in darkness saw great light; and to them which sat in the region and shadow of death light is sprung up." (Matthew 4:16, KJV)

You do not need a prettier form of numbness.

You do not need religious management.

You do not need a polished version of deadness.

You need visitation.

You need awakening.

You need the Shepherd to restore your soul.

"He restoreth my soul: he leadeth me in the paths of righteousness for his name's sake." (Psalm 23:3, KJV)

What hell numbed, the Holy Ghost can awaken.

What hell dehumanized, Christ can restore.

What hell taught you to tolerate does not have to keep ruling you.

And if the Holy Spirit is working to heal your soul, you will notice because the sin that no longer bothered you will start to bother you again. You will start to feel the consequences again. You will start to feel grief where there once was numbness, conviction where there once was permission, and sorrow where there once was deadness. That is not regression. That is mercy. That is evidence that the soul is waking up.

"Who being past feeling have given themselves over unto lasciviousness..." (Ephesians 4:19, KJV)

When a person is past feeling, that is danger. But when feeling begins to return under the work of the Holy Spirit, that is not weakness. That is recovery beginning. That is why a broken and contrite heart is not a bad sign before God. It is a healing sign.

"The sacrifices of God are a broken spirit: a broken and a contrite heart, O God, thou wilt not despise." (Psalm 51:17, KJV)

But the weakness around that sin may remain a vulnerable place in your life for a long time, because your soul was trained to accept what it should have resisted. Your inhibition toward that sin may be weak for a season because the warning system in your soul was damaged. Sin hardens over time (Hebrews 3:13). A conscience can be seared (1 Timothy 4:2). The flesh still wars against the Spirit (Galatians 5:16-17). That is why you must not treat early recovery like finished strength. You must stay honest, stay guarded, and stay yielded while the Holy Spirit retrains what darkness taught your soul to tolerate.

"But exhort one another daily... lest any of you be hardened through the deceitfulness of sin." (Hebrews 3:13, KJV)

So when conviction returns, when grief returns, when your conscience starts feeling again, do not despise that pain. That pain is not your enemy. It is evidence that numbness is breaking. It is evidence that your soul is no longer lying there dead to what once should have troubled it. It is evidence that healing, recovery, and deliverance are beginning.

So stop protecting the dull place.

Stop excusing the numb place.

Stop defending the damaged place.

Bring it into the light.

Because once the soul opens, the remedy has somewhere to land.

Scripture Index:

- Matthew 4:16
- Matthew 13:15
- Luke 4:18
- John 7:38

- Psalm 23:3
- Psalm 51:17
- Proverbs 4:23
- Romans 1:21
- Romans 12:2
- 1 Corinthians 6:9-10
- Galatians 5:16-17
- Galatians 5:19-21
- 2 Corinthians 6:11-12
- Ephesians 4:18-19
- 2 Thessalonians 2:7
- Hebrews 3:13
- Hebrews 5:11-14
- Isaiah 6:10
- 1 Timothy 4:2
- James 3:5-6
- James 1:26
- Proverbs 6:16-19
- Matthew 12:36-37
- John 8:34
- 2 Peter 2:19
- Romans 1:29-32
- Titus 3:10-11

Chapter Six

Appetites: Glorified or Demonized

Introduction: Every Appetite Will Serve a Kingdom

Every appetite in you will serve a kingdom.

It will not remain neutral. It will not stay decorative. It will not sit quietly in the background of your life like a harmless preference while you rename it taste, stress, chemistry, loneliness, personality, trauma, or need. Appetite is not passive. Appetite is power waiting for government. If the Spirit governs it, it rises into design. If darkness governs it, it descends into corruption.

God made you with appetite. He made you with hunger, longing, desire, delight, pursuit, capacity, and the ability to receive. The appetite for food is not evil by itself. The appetite for pleasure is not evil by itself. The appetite for intimacy is not evil by itself. Appetite is not automatically holy, and it is not automatically unholy. It is amoral until a kingdom takes hold of it. Then it becomes glorified or demonized.

That is why this subject cannot be handled softly.

Satan knows exactly how to work this ground. He uses appetite to dehumanize people and destroy them. He takes what was meant to become worship and turns it into craving. He takes what was meant to become covenant and turns it into compulsion. He takes what was meant to become clean delight and turns it into inward demand. He takes what was meant to become holy enjoyment and turns it into an altar for the flesh.

If you do not delight yourself in the Lord, you will start feeling around in the dark for something to fill your soul.

"Delight thyself also in the LORD; and he shall give thee the desires of thine heart." (Psalm 37:4, KJV)

You will search for relief where you were meant to find communion. You will search for sensation where you were meant to find satisfaction. You will search for appetite to tell you what your heart wants because you have lost the place where desire gets interpreted by God.

Every appetite in you will serve a kingdom.

So the question is not whether you have appetites.

The question is whether your appetites answer to the King.

God-Given Appetite Is Not the Problem

God-given appetite is not the problem.

Ungoverned appetite is the problem.

People blame appetite for what surrender was supposed to settle. They blame desire for what obedience was supposed to govern. They blame hunger for what the cross was supposed to crucify. But God did not call you to become less human by pretending you have no desire. He called you to become rightly ordered by bringing desire under heaven's government.

That is why Scripture does not tell you to deny the existence of desire. It tells you to present your body a living sacrifice and be transformed by the renewing of your mind. It tells you to cast down imaginations and bring every thought into captivity to the obedience of Christ. The issue is not whether desire exists. The issue is whether desire rules.

"I beseech you therefore, brethren, by the mercies of God, that ye present your bodies a living sacrifice, holy, acceptable unto God, which is your reasonable service. And be not conformed to this world: but be ye transformed by the renewing of your mind..." (Romans 12:1-2, KJV)

"Casting down imaginations, and every high thing that exalteth itself against the knowledge of God, and bringing into captivity every thought to the obedience of Christ;" (2 Corinthians 10:5, KJV)

Free will is what makes this dangerous. Man was given the capacity to rise or descend. The soul is not static. It is not parked. It is not frozen. It can move upward into likeness, or downward into corruption. That means appetite is never just appetite. It is always becoming something. It is always being trained. It is always being interpreted. It is always moving toward glorification or demonization.

So stop lying on God about what He created.

God did not make you bound.

God did not make you crooked.

God did not make you ruled by urges you excuse but never confront.

God did not make you hidden.

And God did not make you "just this way" when "this way" is clearly the soul's damaged response to fear, shame, rebellion, or appetite.

The problem is not that desire exists.

The problem is that desire keeps trying to sit on a throne it was never meant to occupy.

The Soul Decides What Appetite Becomes

The soul decides what appetite becomes.

That is where this turns dangerous.

You are a spirit. You have a soul. You live in an animal body.

"And the very God of peace sanctify you wholly; and I pray God your whole spirit and soul and body be preserved blameless unto the coming of our Lord Jesus Christ." (1 Thessalonians 5:23, KJV)

No matter how you dress it up, perfume it up, color it up, educate it up, decorate it up, medicate it up, or flatter it up, you are still carrying desire through a soul that has history. Appetite does not bypass that history. It moves through it.

And your flesh does not care if you go to heaven.

Your flesh does not care if you go to hell.

It is going nowhere with God.

That is why the soul matters so much. Appetite does not move through your life untouched. It passes through your mind, will, emotions, conscience, memory, imagination, personality, and inward history.

Then people call the distortion identity.

No.

It is appetite passing through damage.

A wounded soul misreads desire. A fearful soul hides inside desire. A bitter soul uses desire as revenge. A darkened soul argues for desire. A religious soul mislabels desire. A desensitized soul uses desire as anesthesia. And if the soul is bent, appetite does not come out clean.

That is why many people are not meeting the real you.

They are meeting your soul damage.

They are meeting your bruise, your shut-down places, your hidden resentment, your untreated history, your old agreements, your inward fracture, and your unresolved reactions through which appetite is flowing.

The soul does not merely feel appetite.

The soul helps decide what appetite becomes.

"Keep thy heart with all diligence; for out of it are the issues of life." (Proverbs 4:23, KJV)

The issue is not only what you desire.

The issue is what is interpreting your desire.

Appetites Can Be Governed by the Spirit or Hijacked by Darkness

There are only two outcomes here.

Your appetites will either be governed by the Spirit or hijacked by darkness.

When a person lives in union with the Holy Ghost, appetite comes under higher government. Desire is no longer left alone to interpret itself. Hunger is no longer allowed to crown itself king. The Spirit sets order. He teaches restraint. He retrains longing. He cleanses what appetite touches. He turns what would have become compulsion into clean strength.

But if the Spirit is not governing, darkness will.

Darkness studies what your soul will tolerate. It works through compromise until compromise becomes access. It works through access until access becomes traffic. It works through traffic until traffic becomes bondage.

That is how people slide.

Not all at once.

By toleration.

By repetition.

By adaptation.

By desensitization.

Then the soul starts defending what it once would have resisted.

And whatever conditions are in your soul will flavor what flows out of you. If the soul is muddy, the flow gets colored on the way through. If the soul is bent, expression comes out bent. If the soul is wounded, appetite comes out wounded.

That is why polite flesh is still flesh.

Church-trained flesh is still flesh.

Managed flesh is still flesh.

Domesticated flesh is still flesh.

A domesticated animal is still an animal.

The cross was not given to improve the beast.

It was given to kill it.

"And they that are Christ's have crucified the flesh with the affections and lusts." (Galatians 5:24, KJV)

If the flesh is not crucified, it will drag your appetites downward until you start tolerating what once would have made you recoil. And once you start tolerating what heaven calls crooked, you are already moving.

"This I say then, Walk in the Spirit, and ye shall not fulfil the lust of the flesh. For the flesh lusteth against the Spirit, and the Spirit against the flesh: and these are contrary the one to the other..." (Galatians 5:16-17, KJV)

The war is not imaginary. The conflict is real.

Repeated Sin Turns Desire into Bondage

Sin does not stay where it starts.

It moves.

It repeats.

It wraps.

It binds.

Sin begins as action. Then action becomes repeated trespass in the same place, through the same opening, around the same appetite, under the same excuse. Repeated sin does not stay at the level of behavior. It starts building a groove in the soul.

At first you think you are choosing it.

Later it starts choosing the hour.

The lonely hour.

The angry hour.

The tired hour.

The private hour.

The disappointed hour.

The bitter hour.

The weak hour.

That is bondage.

James says every man is drawn away of his own lust, enticed, and then sin brings forth death. That death does not wait for the grave. It starts working in the inward man now.

"But every man is tempted, when he is drawn away of his own lust, and enticed. Then when lust hath conceived, it bringeth forth sin: and sin, when it is finished, bringeth forth death." (James 1:14-15, KJV)

Think of sewing thread wrapped around the same fingers. Two or three wraps can be broken. Twenty or thirty wraps around the same place become binding. That is how repeated sin works. It circles the same appetite until appetite becomes trained captivity.

And yet bondage still knows it is bondage.

That is why people in bondage can still cry out.

They often still know something is wrong.

They still know this is bad.

They still know this is not freedom.

So do not make peace with it.

Repeated sin is training desire in the wrong direction. It is teaching appetite to speak with authority. It is teaching craving to impersonate identity.

"Let not sin therefore reign in your mortal body, that ye should obey it in the lusts thereof. Neither yield ye your members as instruments of unrighteousness unto sin..." (Romans 6:12-13, KJV)

Appetite is always trying to become rule.

Iniquity Is When the Soul Calls Evil Good

Iniquity is worse than rebellion.

Rebellion knows it is wrong and does it anyway.

Iniquity becomes crooked enough to call wrong right.

That is the terrifying stage.

This is where the soul stops merely indulging darkness and starts defending it. It explains it. It decorates it. It justifies it. It asks other people to honor it. The person does not merely sin. The person starts interpreting sin as wisdom, identity, liberation, maturity, or necessity.

That is when the bend becomes interpretive.

That is when appetite starts issuing permission slips.

That is when desire starts writing theology.

That is when the flesh starts preaching.

And once appetite starts preaching, people do not just fall.

They evangelize their fall.

They demand agreement with their fall.

They call their fall freedom.

"Woe unto them that call evil good, and good evil..." (Isaiah 5:20, KJV)

That is why deception is harder to break than open rebellion. A person in rebellion may still be pierced by conviction. A person in deception starts calling conviction oppression, holiness cruelty, correction abuse, and truth hate.

And when the bend reaches that point, the animal is not merely acting.

It is thinking for you.

You were not thinking.

The animal was thinking.

Bent things do not straighten themselves by self-approval.

They must be contradicted by truth.

They must be brought into light.

They must come under the rule of the Spirit.

Self-Control Is a Fruit, Not a Personality Trait

Self-control is not a personality trait.

It is a fruit of the Spirit.

"But the fruit of the Spirit is love, joy, peace, longsuffering, gentleness, goodness, faith, meekness, temperance..." (Galatians 5:22-23, KJV)

That means no man masters this chaos by natural strength. You cannot control this monster called the humanistic soul and the flesh without the Holy Ghost. You cannot educate the beast into holiness. You cannot flatter yourself into freedom. You cannot simply promise your way out of appetite's tyranny.

The flesh does not care if you go to heaven.

The flesh does not care if you go to hell.

It is not trying to become holy.

That is why the Church has to stop confusing niceness with holiness. A church that refuses to confront sin does not create safety. It creates polished captivity. Conviction is not cruelty. Exposure is not meanness. Government is not abuse.

And underneath all of this is one practical issue: self-government.

If there is no self-government, families fail.

If there is no self-government, churches fail.

If there is no self-government, societies fail.

If there is no self-government, nations fail.

Any system without inward government eventually collapses under the pressure of unruled appetite.

This is why even born-again people can still live with chaotic souls. A person can be genuinely saved and still have an out-of-control soul if that soul never comes under the government of the Spirit. Tongues by themselves do not prove the soul is governed. Gifting by itself does not prove appetite is clean. Emotion by itself does not prove maturity.

Self-control means passion is no longer allowed to run wild and call itself sincerity. It means sensual appetite is mastered, reaction is curbed, and balance is restored under the rule of the Spirit. It means the soul stops agreeing with darkness and starts answering to God.

This is not behavior management.

This is government.

This is heaven getting its seat back.

"But I keep under my body, and bring it into subjection..." (1 Corinthians 9:27, KJV)

That is not symbolic language.

That is disciplined government.

Conclusion: Ungoverned Appetite Always Ends in Ruin

Ungoverned appetite always ends in ruin.

Always.

Sometimes the ruin is loud. Sometimes it is slow. Sometimes it wrecks a marriage. Sometimes it hollows out a conscience. Sometimes it poisons a mind. Sometimes it rots a ministry. Sometimes it wounds a family line. Sometimes it deforms a soul until the person can no longer feel correctly, choose correctly, or discern correctly.

So stop flattering what should be crucified.

Stop excusing what should be governed.

Stop calling bondage honesty.

Stop calling compulsion identity.

Stop calling domesticated flesh transformation.

Stop calling low-level captivity peace.

Stop calling a dull soul normal.

Stop calling polished captivity maturity.

And ask the Holy Ghost a harder question than most people are willing to ask.

Have I been dehumanized?

Have I been desensitized?

Has my soul tolerated what it should have rejected?

Has appetite been serving a lower kingdom while I kept giving it softer names?

Has the beast been thinking for me?

Because something is ruling.

That is the issue.

And the answer is not better management of the beast.

The answer is death to the beast, sanctification of the soul, and government by the Spirit. The Word of God was not given to flatter appetite. It was given to bring every thought, every desire, every impulse, and every inward movement back under Christ.

God did not make you for demonic appetite.

He made you for ordered desire.

He made you for glorified appetite.

He made you for a soul that can receive cleanly, answer rightly, and come back under heaven's rule again.

Every appetite in you will serve a kingdom.

Make sure it serves the King.

Scripture Index:

- Psalm 37:4
- Proverbs 4:23
- Isaiah 5:20
- Romans 6:12-13
- Romans 12:1-2
- 1 Corinthians 9:27
- 2 Corinthians 10:5
- Galatians 5:16-17
- Galatians 5:22-24
- James 1:14-15
- 1 Thessalonians 5:23

Part III

The Return of Perception

A damaged soul does not only hurt. It misreads. It mistakes. It resists what it should receive and receives what it should resist. This section turns toward countenance, dullness, discernment, unforgiveness, and the recovery of perception itself. The burden here is sharp because the loss here is severe: if the soul loses the power to perceive, it loses the power to receive. Frozen feeling must thaw. Crooked judgment must be straightened. The inward eye must open again. God is not merely comforting the damaged man here. He is restoring the power to recognize truth, receive help, feel rightly, and stop calling darkness normal.

"Open thou mine eyes, that I may behold wondrous things out of thy law." (Psalm 119:18, KJV)

Chapter Seven

Your Face is Telling on You

Introduction: The Soul Does Not Stay Hidden Forever

You can hide for a while.

You can hide behind vocabulary.

You can hide behind church behavior.

You can hide behind makeup, clothing, style, posture, humor, silence, knowledge, gifting, smiling, distance, busyness, politeness, and religious performance.

But the soul does not stay hidden forever.

Sooner or later, what the soul is carrying starts showing.

It shows in the countenance.

It shows in the eyes.

It shows in the weight of the face.

It shows in the reaction time.

It shows in the tightness, the dullness, the hardness, the brightness, the grief, the strain, the openness, the warmth, the coldness, the suspicion, the inward collapse, the unrest, or the peace resting on a person.

That is why this chapter matters.

People think the soul is invisible because it is inward. It is inward, but it is not without evidence. The face becomes a witness. The countenance becomes a testimony. What a person has been living in begins to write itself outwardly. You can only carry contradiction so long before your face starts helping tell the story.

Your face is telling on you.

That is not condemnation.

That is revelation.

The countenance is one of the places where the hidden life becomes visible.

The Bible Calls It Countenance

The Bible does not treat the face like a minor detail.

It treats it like a witness.

It calls it countenance.

"A merry heart maketh a cheerful countenance: but by sorrow of the heart the spirit is broken." (Proverbs 15:13, KJV)

That verse alone tells you something important. The face is not random. It is not disconnected from the inward man. A merry heart makes a cheerful countenance. Sorrow in the heart breaks the spirit and marks the outward man. That means the face is not merely skin. It is an outlet. It is a carrier. It is a visible expression of what is going on inside the soul.

Then Scripture says:

"Who is as the wise man? and who knoweth the interpretation of a thing? a man's wisdom maketh his face to shine, and the boldness of his face shall be changed." (Ecclesiastes 8:1, KJV)

Wisdom affects the face.

The inward life affects the face.

The spirit a person lives in affects the face.

That is why countenance matters. The face is not the whole story, but it is often a true witness. It may not tell you everything immediately, but it tells you something. It can tell you whether peace is present, whether bitterness is feeding, whether fear is ruling, whether joy is alive, whether sorrow is breaking the spirit, whether wisdom is shining, or whether darkness has been living there too long.

The soul leaves marks.

And the face helps carry them.

What Is in the Soul Starts Showing Outwardly

A person can say one thing with the mouth and another thing with the face.

That is why countenance matters so much.

You can say, "I'm fine," while your face says trouble.

You can say, "I forgive them," while your face says the wound is still hot.

You can say, "I trust God," while your face says fear is ruling the room.

You can say, "I'm happy for them," while your face says envy just walked in.

You can say, "I'm not angry," while your face is already testifying against you.

That is because the soul keeps leaking evidence.

What is inside eventually starts showing outside.

This is one of the reasons darkness loves religious performance. Performance can train the mouth faster than it trains the soul. It can make a person sound right before they are right. It can make them learn the language of health while the inward man is still carrying agitation, offense, pride, fear, victimhood, secrecy, or grief that has not been healed. But countenance often tells the truth faster than speech does.

That does not mean you become a professional face-reader and start acting spooky. It means you stop pretending the soul has no visible evidence.

The soul has visible evidence.

The countenance is one of them.

Your Face Tells on What You Have Been Living In

What you have been living in writes on you.

That is one of the hardest truths for people to accept.

They want to believe they can live in inward chaos without outward testimony.

They want to believe they can harbor bitterness, envy, pride, lust, victimhood, and unresolved trouble without it marking anything.

But over time, the soul starts teaching the face how to testify.

There are people who look more peaceful than they speak.

There are people who look more troubled than they admit.

There are people who look brighter because wisdom is working.

There are people who look harder because pride has been ruling too long.

There are people whose whole countenance has begun to bend around what they live in.

That is why some people say, "I just took a liking to that person," and they cannot fully explain why. Sometimes the face is already carrying evidence of peace, wisdom, honesty, and inward order. And sometimes the opposite is also true. Sometimes people recoil and cannot explain why. The face is already carrying evidence of unrest, hidden hostility, suspicion, inward fracture, or defilement.

The face does not tell everything.

But it tells something.

And often it tells enough to know that the soul is carrying a story.

Under Forty, Over Forty

There is a blunt truth here that lands hard because it is true.

Under a certain age, much of what you see is simply the face a person was born with.

But as time goes on, what they have been living in starts writing itself there.

That is why a person can age and not merely look older, but look more like what they have been feeding.

Anger has a look.

Bitterness has a look.

Victimhood has a look.

Fear has a look.

Peace has a look.

Wisdom has a look.

The face starts learning the spirit a person lives in.

Some people are more exhausted in their countenance than in their schedule.

Some are more broken in their face than in their words.

Some look harsher because the soul has been feeding on harshness for years.

Some look shut down because the soul has lived in hiding too long.

Some look lighter because truth has been working in the inward man.

Again, this is not about vanity.

This is about witness.

Your countenance is telling on what has been shaping you.

The Eyes and Face Are Windows of the Soul

People say the eyes are the window of the soul because there is truth to that.

The face gives away what the mouth tries to manage.

The eyes tell you when a person is open, cold, alive, numb, soft, defensive, dark, peaceful, or internally divided. The soul is inward, but the eyes and countenance often reveal whether life is flowing cleanly or getting obstructed.

That is why a closed soul often carries a closed face.

And a troubled soul often carries troubled eyes.

A person can walk into a room and look straight through people because inwardly they are disconnected. They are not present. They are guarded. They are armored. They are shut. They are there physically, but the soul is not answering openly.

That is why the face matters. It often reveals whether a person is receiving, resisting, hiding, grieving, or dull.

"The light of the body is the eye: if therefore thine eye be single, thy whole body shall be full of light." (Matthew 6:22, KJV)

A single eye affects the whole body.

A darkened eye affects the whole body.

That means the face is not a throwaway detail. Heaven pays attention to what is coming through the eye and what is showing through the countenance.

A Merry Heart and a Broken Spirit Do Not Look the Same

"A merry heart maketh a cheerful countenance: but by sorrow of the heart the spirit is broken." (Proverbs 15:13, KJV)

That means inward life has visible consequence.

A merry heart does not merely stay invisible and private. It brightens. It affects. It shows. Real joy has outward evidence. It is not always loud, but it is alive. It has light in it. It has warmth in it. It has openness in it. It has ease in it.

And sorrow of heart does not merely remain conceptual either. It breaks the spirit. It weighs the face down. It drains color from the inward life. It can make the countenance heavy even when the person is trying to sound fine.

That is why unresolved soul damage cannot be treated like a harmless private burden. It leaks into visible life. It changes how a person receives, responds, and appears. It begins affecting relationships, opportunities, trust, and how other people experience their presence.

This is not about superficial image.

This is about inward condition producing outward evidence.

Wisdom Changes the Face

Wisdom is not only informational.

It is transformational.

It affects the face.

"A man's wisdom maketh his face to shine..." (Ecclesiastes 8:1, KJV)

That is one of the great promises hidden in this chapter. The face does not only testify against trouble. It can testify for wisdom. The countenance can brighten when order comes in. The face can change when the soul comes under truth. A person who has lived in darkness is not trapped forever under the same expression. If wisdom begins working, the face can begin changing. If truth begins governing, the countenance can begin shifting. If the soul begins healing, the outward witness can start telling a different story.

That means this chapter is not merely diagnostic.

It is hopeful.

God can change what has been written there by what He is healing inside. He can put brightness where there was dullness. He can put peace where there was strain. He can put openness where there was fear. He can put warmth where there was hardness. He can put life where there was deadness.

Wisdom affects the face because wisdom affects the soul.

Brokenness, Bitterness, and Victimhood Start Showing

Some of the strongest visible distortions come from bitterness, sorrow, and victimhood.

A person can live in grievance so long that the grievance begins to inhabit the face. They do not merely remember what happened. They wear what happened. Their whole countenance starts bending around their offense. The injury becomes interpretive. Then every relationship starts getting filtered through that same bruise.

This is why some people look aggravated before they speak.

Some look offended before anything has happened.

Some look suspicious before anyone even touches the issue.

The face is already telling on the wound.

That does not mean you condemn people by appearance. It means you take seriously that the soul is leaving evidence. A bitter soul often cannot hide completely. A victim mentality often starts writing itself visibly. A person can carry so much unresolved inward pressure that even in silence, the countenance keeps giving witness.

Scripture warns about bitterness springing up and defiling many.

"Looking diligently lest any man fail of the grace of God; lest any root of bitterness springing up trouble you, and thereby many be defiled;" (Hebrews 12:15, KJV)

Roots hidden in the soul eventually produce fruit visible in life.

Countenance is one of those visible places.

Do Not Lose Your Perception, Reception, and Countenance

There is a connection between disobedience, dullness, and visible evidence.

If the soul keeps tolerating what it should resist, it dulls perception.

If perception dulls, reception weakens.

If reception weakens, life starts feeling far away.

That is why people say, "I know the promise is there, but it seems far away."

The issue is not always that God moved.

The issue is often that the soul has become dull.

And if the soul becomes dull long enough, it starts affecting the face, the eyes, the reactions, the atmosphere around the person, and the way they carry themselves in ordinary life.

Everything that comes to you in the spirit requires perception before reception. If the soul is darkened, what should be received cleanly gets misread. And when the soul lives like that too long, the countenance starts bearing witness to the inner confusion.

That is why it is dangerous to keep the soul cluttered. You are not only risking inward confusion. You are risking outward testimony. The face starts helping tell people what spirit has been shaping you.

Seek His Face, and Your Face Changes

The answer to a damaged countenance is not cosmetic.

It is not image management.

It is not learning a better church smile.

It is not practicing softer body language while the inward man remains untouched.

The answer is the face of God.

"When thou saidst, Seek ye my face; my heart said unto thee, Thy face, LORD, will I seek." (Psalm 27:8, KJV)

What you seek reshapes you.

If you keep seeking offense, your face will learn offense.

If you keep seeking lust, your face will learn lust.

If you keep seeking fear, your face will learn fear.

If you keep seeking grievance, your face will learn grievance.

But if you seek His face, your face starts changing under His rule.

This is the hidden mercy of the chapter. The same countenance that has been telling on soul damage can begin telling on healing. The face can begin carrying peace. The eyes can begin carrying light. The expression can begin carrying truth. The visible witness can start changing because the inward man is no longer feeding on the same darkness.

"But we all, with open face beholding as in a glass the glory of the Lord, are changed..." (2 Corinthians 3:18, KJV)

Open face.

Changed.

That is not just theology.

That is transformation with visible consequence.

Conclusion: Your Face Is a Witness

Your face is a witness.

Your countenance is a witness.

Your eyes are a witness.

Your reactions are a witness.

What you have been living in is speaking.

The question is: what is it saying?

Is it saying peace?

Is it saying grief?

Is it saying wisdom?

Is it saying bitterness?

Is it saying dullness?

Is it saying fear?

Is it saying joy?

Is it saying inward fracture?

Is it saying the soul is open?

Or is it saying something inside has been shut too long?

This is not written to make people self-conscious.

It is written to make them truthful.

Because when the soul is healed, the countenance changes.

When wisdom enters, the face begins to shine.

When bitterness breaks, the heaviness starts lifting.

When the broken spirit is restored, the face stops carrying the same testimony.

When the inward man comes under light, the visible man starts bearing a different witness.

That is why this chapter matters.

Your face is telling on you.

Let it start telling the truth of healing.

Scripture Index:

- Proverbs 15:13
- Ecclesiastes 8:1
- Matthew 6:22
- Psalm 27:8
- Hebrews 12:15
- 2 Corinthians 3:18
- Psalm 34:5
- Genesis 4:5-6
- 1 Samuel 1:18
- Nehemiah 2:2
- Isaiah 3:9
- Luke 9:51

Chapter Eight

Perception Before Reception

Introduction: You Cannot Receive What You Cannot Perceive

Everything that comes to you in the Spirit requires perception before reception.

If you cannot perceive it, you cannot receive it.

That is not a slogan. That is law. The soul does not receive holy things by accident. It receives them by discernment. When perception is damaged, reception is damaged. That is why people can sit near real things and still never enter their benefit. They can watch power move and leave saying, "I wonder what that was." They saw motion, but they never recognized visitation. They sat near life, but they never entered what life was offering.

That is one of the cruelest forms of soul damage. A person can stay near real things and still never enter their benefit. They can watch power move and leave saying, "I wonder what that was." They saw activity but did not recognize access. They heard truth but did not identify its value. They were close geographically and still far spiritually.

Promise can feel far away when it is not far away.

Healing can feel far away when it is not far away.

Joy can feel far away when it is not far away.

The distance is not always in God.

Many times the distance is in perception.

"Open thou mine eyes, that I may behold wondrous things out of thy law." (Psalm 119:18, KJV)

That is not a prayer for information only.

It is a prayer for sight.

Open my eyes.

Let me behold.

Let me perceive.

Let me stop living around holy things like a stranger to them.

Everything in the Spirit Requires Perception First

We belong to an invisible Kingdom with outward manifestation. You cannot see the Holy Ghost with natural eyes. You have to perceive Him. You have to recognize what He is pressing, what He is opening, what He is exposing, what He is offering, and what He is calling for in the moment.

Two people can sit under the same word, in the same atmosphere, and leave with completely different outcomes. One perceived and received. The other observed and wondered. One recognized that God was dealing with them and yielded. The other noticed movement in the room but never entered the transaction.

A healing does not float through the room with a sign hanging over it.

Deliverance does not always announce itself in a way the dull soul can interpret.

The Holy Ghost can move, chains can break, devils can lose territory, truth can come alive, and a person can still sit there unmoved because the inward man no longer knows how to identify holy advantage.

"The light of the body is the eye: if therefore thine eye be single, thy whole body shall be full of light. But if thine eye be evil, thy whole body shall be full of darkness..." (Matthew 6:22-23, KJV)

Christ tied sight to the whole condition of the person.

That means this is not a side issue.

If sight is damaged, life gets misread.

If life gets misread, then opportunities get mishandled, warnings get ignored, mercies get overlooked, and the soul keeps walking past what heaven was actually giving.

Why Many People Stay Near the Kingdom but Never Enter Its Benefit

Some people want the benefits of the Kingdom while resisting the conditions of the Kingdom.

They want favor without forsaking.

They want comfort without correction.

They want breakthrough without responsibility.

They want healing without surrender.

They want vertical inspiration, but not horizontal obedience.

Vertical preaching usually does not get you in trouble. Aim the barrel high and everybody is happy because they see fireworks. They get emotional. They get excited. They shout, respond, and enjoy the upward sound of it. The message goes high, and because it is not yet turning straight into their personal issues, they can celebrate it without feeling threatened.

Lower the barrel some, and people start getting a little nervous.

But put that barrel on horizontal, and many people get scared and mad, because now the message is no longer just going upward in inspiring language. Now it is coming straight into conduct, speech, attitudes, loyalties, hidden compromise, personal issues, damaged reactions, private appetites, family order, money order, relationship order, and the things they do not want touched. They do not mind a feel-good message. They just do not want a change message.

That is where many stop receiving.

Not because God stopped giving.

Because they stopped wanting what He was giving.

The soul can enjoy spiritual atmosphere and still hate spiritual government.

That is why people stay near church while losing benefit. They want God on discount. They want favor while withholding surrender. They want the fruit of obedience while still negotiating private terms.

"So likewise, whosoever he be of you that forsaketh not all that he hath, he cannot be my disciple." (Luke 14:33, KJV)

That means there is no clarity for what you insist on protecting.

No sharpness for what you insist on preserving against God.

No clean sight where the soul is still bargaining.

You can still be moving and lose the benefit. Like driving to Florida with no air conditioning, the car still runs, but the ride becomes miserable because benefit was lost. Transportation is one thing. Benefit is another. Motion is one thing. Reception is another.

Closed Eyes Create a Dull Soul

Jesus did not describe these people as lacking eyes.

He described them as having eyes they closed.

That means much of dullness is not accidental. It is chosen. The soul closes its eyes to truth, to correction, to responsibility, to what God already made plain, and then acts confused when perception starts fading.

"For this people's heart is waxed gross, and their ears are dull of hearing, and their eyes they have closed..." (Matthew 13:15, KJV)

The language is severe because the condition is severe.

Thick.

Calloused.

Stupefied.

Rendered dull and lacking perception.

A soul can become so repeatedly resistant that it no longer knows how to draw near cleanly. The eyes are still there, but the capacity to receive through them has been weakened by repeated refusal.

"Make the heart of this people fat, and make their ears heavy, and shut their eyes..." (Isaiah 6:10, KJV)

That is not harmless immaturity.

That is a damaged inward life defending its own blindness.

You say, "Why do you talk so strong?"

Because perception is too expensive to lose.

A clean heart can handle strong preaching.

A compromised heart calls strong preaching cruelty because dullness has already taught it to fear whatever still cuts straight.

Disobedience Dulls Discernment

Disobedience is expensive because it does not only cost peace.

It costs perception.

You cannot shut your eyes over here and still expect to see clearly over there. That is not how it works. God is not making requests. He is making commands. And when He asks for something, He does not need your committee review, your emotional vote, or your delayed cooperation.

Then later people wonder why they got fooled, why they got hustled, why they missed the counterfeit, why they could not tell what was clean and what was crooked.

The answer is brutal and plain.

They shut their eyes over here.

That is why partial obedience is not small. It is training. Every delayed yes, every defended compromise, every substitute laid on the altar in place of what God actually required is training the soul to lose sharpness.

Do not act like this only costs favor.

It costs advantage.

If I lose the power of perception, I lose the benefit of reception, but I am still hungry. That is why people start living on substitutes. They lose the power to recognize what God was giving them anymore, but the soul is still craving life, so now it starts feeding on what only imitates life.

"Be ye doers of the word, and not hearers only, deceiving your own selves." (James 1:22, KJV)

Hearing without obedience trains deception.

And deception always clouds sight.

So hear it plainly.

Do not lose your perception because of your disobedience.

You are not just risking comfort.

You are risking sight.

A Desensitized Soul Cannot Judge Clearly

Once perception is damaged, judgment goes crooked.

A desensitized soul cannot judge clearly because it no longer reads life straight. It misreads love as control. It misreads correction as rejection. It misreads holiness as harshness. It misreads clarity as attack. It misreads strong preaching as abuse. It misreads order because it has lost the power to recognize Kingdom normal.

"Of whom we have many things to say, and hard to be uttered, seeing ye are dull of hearing." (Hebrews 5:11, KJV)

Dullness of hearing does not mean heaven fell silent.

It means the soul lost its power to answer.

That is the danger.

God can still be speaking while the inward man no longer knows how to respond. The room can still be full of possibility while the soul remains locked outside its own benefit. The person stays hungry, but they are no longer interpreting reality correctly.

"Having the understanding darkened, being alienated from the life of God through the ignorance that is in them, because of the blindness of their heart:" (Ephesians 4:18, KJV)

That is why some people are hard to help even when they say they want help. The help has to come through the soul. The soul has to be open. But when the inward man is dulled, cluttered, desensitized, and darkened, it does not answer rightly.

Do not call that maturity.

Do not call that balance.

Do not call that being unbothered.

That is injury left untreated long enough to impersonate personality.

The Loss of Perception Is the Loss of Advantage

Perception is one of the great advantages of the restored soul.

If you lose that, you lose more than feeling.

You lose warning.

You lose timing.

You lose clarity.

You lose the ability to spot the trap before it closes.

You lose the power to distinguish value.

You lose the clean inward witness that says, "This is right," or, "This is crooked."

That is how people get taken by hustlers.

That is how they get cheated in broad daylight.

That is how they sit near truth and still miss the benefit.

Some people are not far from truth geographically.

They are far from truth perceptually.

That is why the loss is so severe. You may still attend. You may still speak Christian language. You may still call yourself committed. You may still be moving in a basic sense. But if perception is gone, advantage is gone.

That is not peace.

That is dullness with a church vocabulary.

The loss of perception is the loss of advantage.

You may still be moving, but you are moving late.

You may still believe, but believe foggily.

You may still attend, but keep missing what was meant for you.

You may still sit near the table and still starve.

Counterfeit Replaces What You Failed to Perceive

When the soul stops perceiving rightly, it does not stop hungering.

That is why counterfeit becomes so dangerous.

A person still wants life, still wants comfort, still wants meaning, still wants relief, still wants purpose, still wants to feel whole. But if they can no longer recognize the real thing, they start bonding to replacements.

Counterfeit relief.

Counterfeit love.

Counterfeit purpose.

Counterfeit identity.

Counterfeit peace.

Counterfeit spirituality.

That is why substitutes become so persuasive to a dull soul. The hunger is still there, but the discernment is damaged.

"And no marvel; for Satan himself is transformed into an angel of light." (2 Corinthians 11:14, KJV)

If counterfeit can present itself as light, then damaged sight is no small issue.

If the eye is not clean, the soul will keep mistaking imitation for substance.

That is how people start feeding on what wounds them while calling it wisdom.

That is how they call compromise peace.

That is how they call bondage identity.

That is how they call darkness maturity.

Conclusion: What God Opens Must Be Kept Open

If He opens your eyes, do not shut them again. If He exposes where you have been dull, do not rename it balance. If He shows you where disobedience clouded your discernment, do not protect it. If He reveals where substitutes took over because you stopped perceiving the real thing, do not negotiate with them.

Perception is too expensive to lose.

Some people cannot recover clarity because too much mess is living in the soul. They can read more books, attend more meetings, chase more language, and still remain dull because the stuff in the soul was never crucified, never confessed, never confronted, and never brought under light.

This has to become the cry again:

I want my perception back.

Not a prettier excuse.

Not a softer compromise.

Not a polished version of dullness.

My perception back.

"Open thou mine eyes, that I may behold wondrous things out of thy law." (Psalm 119:18, KJV)

Open my eyes to the Kingdom.

Open my ears to correction.

Open my heart to responsibility.

Open my soul to truth.

Because if I cannot perceive, I cannot receive.

Scripture Index:

- Psalm 119:18
- Isaiah 6:10
- Matthew 6:22-23
- Matthew 13:15
- Luke 14:33
- Romans 12:2
- Ephesians 4:18
- Hebrews 5:11
- James 1:22
- 2 Corinthians 11:14
- Proverbs 4:23
- John 8:12

Chapter Nine

Forgiveness Restores Feeling

Introduction: The Soul Cannot Heal While Holding Debt

Some damage does not first collapse a life in public.

It freezes it in private.

The years keep moving. The body keeps aging. Routine keeps moving. Church attendance can keep moving. Work can keep moving. But the inward man can remain arrested around an unpaid debt, replaying the same scene, preserving the same indictment, and waiting for payment from people who do not have the power to restore what they broke.

That is why forgiveness is not sentimental.

It is not soft.

It is not a side issue for emotional Christians.

It is a government issue in the soul.

The soul cannot heal while holding debt. It cannot return to clean feeling while still running a private courtroom. Some want peace while preserving bitterness. Some want discernment while protecting offense. Some want healing while guarding accusation. Some want God to touch them while the soul is still gripping fathers, mothers, brothers, sisters, leaders, church people, betrayers, and old versions of themselves by the throat inwardly.

That does not work.

One of the number one things that kills the power of perception is unforgiveness. When perception starts dying, feeling follows it into darkness. A cluttered soul cannot carry a clean flow. A shut heart cannot feel rightly for long. A soul full of old cases cannot stay open before God. There are so many unresolved issues—sin, shame, fear, bitterness, and old injury—that the flow of the Holy Ghost collides with pollution before it can move cleanly through the inward man.

Forgiveness is not merely about what happened between you and another person.

It is about whether your soul remains frozen or returns to life.

"And forgive us our sins; for we also forgive every one that is indebted to us." (Luke 11:4, KJV)

Debt language is not accidental.

Heaven knows exactly what unforgiveness does to the soul.

Unforgiveness Freezes the Inner Life

Unforgiveness keeps injury cold.

It preserves it.

It stores it.

It keeps it on ice.

That is why some people can mention a wound from twenty years ago and instantly become the same person they were when it happened. The calendar moved, but the soul did not.

Their body aged. Their speech matured. Their responsibilities increased. But inwardly they are still standing in the same room making the same accusation and holding the same debt.

Time does not heal what the soul keeps preserving.

Time can age a wound without curing it.

Time can bury pain without healing it.

Time can make you quieter without making you whole.

If something from years ago can still make you rage, recoil, panic, go numb, spiral, or shut down, then time did not heal it. Time merely carried it.

Unforgiveness freezes tenderness.

It freezes trust.

It freezes worship.

It freezes openness.

It freezes courage.

Then people rename the freeze. They call it caution. They call it wisdom. They call it balance. They call it maturity.

No.

It is the inner life sitting in spiritual refrigeration because the offense was never released.

And the damage does not stop at emotion. It begins interfering with perception. If I lose the power of perception, up becomes down, down becomes up, good becomes bad, and bad becomes good. That is not a small loss. That is catastrophic. A person can sit in a room full of help and misread the whole room because the inward lens has gone crooked.

Family wounds cut especially deep. The sins of the brothers always cut deeper because they happen close. That is why some of the hardest people to forgive are fathers, mothers, brothers, sisters, and people tied to blood, memory, and identity. When those wounds are not released, the heart does not merely ache.

It hardens.

And when the heart hardens, perception starts going with it. What should be clear becomes cloudy. What should be received becomes resisted. What should feel clean starts feeling foreign. The soul starts misreading normal as threat. It turns the inward life cold and then lies that the coldness is wisdom.

"But exhort one another daily, while it is called To day; lest any of you be hardened through the deceitfulness of sin." (Hebrews 3:13, KJV)

A hardened heart does not stay tender toward God.

And it does not stay perceptive either.

Bitterness Distorts Relationships, Worship, and Judgment

Bitterness is not just pain.

It is pain with interpretation attached.

It teaches the soul how to read everything after the wound.

That is why bitter people do not only remember what happened. They start filtering life through what happened. New people start paying for old injuries. Current voices get judged by former betrayals. Correction feels hostile. Faithfulness feels controlling. Leadership feels dangerous. Closeness feels manipulative. Even kindness starts feeling suspicious when bitterness has taken over the lens.

You do not see the world the way it is.

You see the world the way you are.

That is not psychology talk.

That is spiritual law.

A bruised place reacts to ordinary touch. A healed scar does not. That is how soul damage works. When a normal moment gets touched and the response comes back far out of proportion, something in the soul is still bleeding. A person can be lightly corrected and erupt. Ordinarily questioned and shut down. Gently approached and instantly withdraw.

That is not discernment.

That is damage reacting.

Church hurt especially works this way. A man can walk into a room who merely resembles a former abuser, a corrupt pastor, or a manipulator from years ago, and people will start answering the new person as though he were the old offender. He is not that man. He just touched the wrong memory. That is what bitterness does. It makes old injuries sit at the door and evaluate every new arrival.

Bitterness distorts worship too. A bitter soul may still sing. It may still pray. It may still quote Scripture. It may still lift its hands. But inwardly it is dragging old verdicts into the presence of God. It is too armed to adore cleanly. Too suspicious to rest. Too cluttered to answer lightly before the Lord.

Then judgment goes crooked with everything else. A dull soul misreads everything. It misreads love as control. It misreads correction as rejection. It misreads holiness as harshness. It misreads clarity as attack. It misreads order because it has lost the ability to recognize Kingdom normal.

Bitterness does not merely hurt the past.

It rewrites the present.

"Looking diligently lest any man fail of the grace of God; lest any root of bitterness springing up trouble you, and thereby many be defiled;" (Hebrews 12:15, KJV)

Roots hidden in the soul eventually start governing visible life.

The Body Carries What the Soul Refuses to Release

What the soul will not surrender, the body starts carrying.

God did not make body, soul, and spirit to live as disconnected compartments. When the inward man cycles anger, resentment, bitterness, hatred, replayed pain, and unresolved grief, the body does not stay untouched. Rest gets affected. Sleep gets affected. Breathing gets affected. Reactions get affected.

Countenance gets affected. The whole frame starts carrying what the soul refused to hand over.

The debt stops being abstract.

The body begins hosting it.

That is why some people cannot settle. They cannot stop replaying. They cannot stop bracing. They cannot stop tightening up in ordinary moments because the soul is still guarding an old injury like sacred property.

Then they start reaching for substitutes. More noise. More appetite. More stimulation. More distraction. More activity. They are trying to feel life because the inward man has gone dull under stored grievance. A desensitized soul still gets hungry. But when it loses the power of perception and feeling, it starts overdoing everything, trying to make the body produce what the soul no longer feels rightly.

That is why people overeat, overdrink, overmedicate, oversexualize, overgamble, overspend, and overstimulate.

The soul is deadened.

The appetites are still alive.

The body gets recruited to solve what only surrender to God can heal.

When the soul gets shut down, people start pushing limits everywhere because they are trying to feel something again. The body becomes a set of jumper cables for a numb inner life. But the body was never designed to resurrect what bitterness has frozen.

"I beseech you therefore, brethren, by the mercies of God, that ye present your bodies a living sacrifice..." (Romans 12:1, KJV)

The body was built to serve righteousness, not to carry the fumes of a private courtroom through the nervous system.

If the soul refuses surrender, the whole person pays.

Why Many People Cannot Feel God Correctly

Many people do not lose all feeling.

They lose right feeling.

They still feel irritation. They still feel suspicion. They still feel self-protection. They still feel anger. They still feel offense. What they lose is clean tenderness toward God. Joy starts feeling far away. Peace starts feeling far away. Communion starts feeling far away. The presence of God starts feeling far away.

But the distance is not always in heaven.

Many times the distance is in the soul.

Some say they want a visitation of the Holy Ghost. Good. Then they must also want what makes visitation possible. It is not church until God shows up. But even when He shows up, a shut soul can stay untouched. A room can hold presence while a wounded heart stays barricaded.

That is the danger.

People can come to a real move of God and still sit there like spectators because their inner world is clogged with unresolved issues. Old accusations are still hanging on the walls.

Church hurt is still alive. Family betrayal is still alive. Shame is still alive. Fear is still alive. Private verdicts are still demanding a hearing. Then when God tries to come through the soul, the flow collides with what was never cleared.

Some people are full of knowledge but have very little life. They know words. They know doctrine. They know church language. But the moment God tries to flow through the inward man, He meets congestion. The soul is so cluttered that even holy movement gets distorted on the way through.

That is why discernment starts failing.

That is why judgment starts bending.

That is why clean things start feeling strange.

That is why strange things start feeling normal.

You cannot close your eyes over here and have perception over there.

It does not work.

If you refuse responsibility where God has already spoken, you do not become deep. You become dull. You do not become guarded. You become clouded. You do not become wise. You become resistant with religious vocabulary.

"For this people's heart is waxed gross, and their ears are dull of hearing, and their eyes they have closed..." (Matthew 13:15, KJV)

That language is severe for a reason.

Thick.

Calloused.

Stupefied.

Dull of hearing.

Lacking perception.

This is not a harmless condition. This is a damaged inner life losing the power to draw a right inference.

And if I cannot perceive, I cannot receive.

Everything in the Spirit requires perception before reception. You cannot receive what your soul has lost the ability to perceive. Without the power of perception, a demonic hustler will capture you and real help will offend you. Without perception, a wolf can feel safe and a shepherd can feel dangerous. Without perception, blessing can arrive in the form of a person and be rejected because the soul misread the package.

That is why some people can sit in real presence and still not enter the benefit. They can attend church, read books, chase impartation, ask for prophecy, and still not receive because the clutter in their soul is killing their ability to perceive.

No Discount for What You Refuse to Surrender

God does not have an auction.

Pay full price or keep walking.

Nothing in the Kingdom goes on sale. Nobody gets a discount because the wound was real. Nobody gets a special because betrayal cut deep. When God says forgive, your arguments are not insight. They are resistance. When He says release it, your explanations are not wisdom. They are negotiation. When He says clear it, your delay is not maturity. It is disobedience dressed in church language.

No favor for what you refuse to surrender.

That line feels hard because heaven does not flatter resistance.

Forgiveness is not optional obedience for elite Christians.

It is baseline government for the soul.

"For if ye forgive men their trespasses, your heavenly Father will also forgive you:" (Matthew 6:14, KJV)

That is not soft language.

That is covenant seriousness.

The Lord's Prayer exposes how serious this is. The one relational issue singled out there is forgiveness. Why? Because unforgiveness shuts down perception. Especially in family. Especially among the close. Especially where love and injury touched the same place.

"For the kingdom of God is not meat and drink; but righteousness, and peace, and joy in the Holy Ghost." (Romans 14:17, KJV)

When unforgiveness fogs the receiver, righteousness, peace, and joy start feeling distant in practice, even though the Kingdom has not moved.

Perception is in the balance.

That is how serious this is.

Forgiveness Returns Sensitivity to the Heart

Forgiveness is not calling evil good.

It is not pretending the wound was small.

It is not denying what happened.

It is refusing to remain chained to it.

Forgiveness is the thawing of the inward man. It is the restoration of holy sensitivity. When forgiveness enters, the heart begins to unclench. The soul stops needing to stay armed every minute. Feeling starts returning in right order. Not sentimental feeling. Not foolish openness.

Clean feeling.

The ability to answer God without old poison hijacking the response. The ability to receive love without assuming manipulation. The ability to hear correction without reacting like it is another betrayal. The ability to worship without dragging old verdicts into the room.

This is where pride has to die.

Because the offended soul always believes it has a special exemption. It says, You do not know what they did to me. That may be true. But the harder question remains. Was what they did to you worse than what your sin did against Christ?

No.

Hell multiplies vengeance.

The Kingdom multiplies release.

Lamech boasted in multiplied vengeance, saying, "*If Cain shall be avenged sevenfold, truly Lamech seventy and sevenfold*" (Genesis 4:24, KJV). However, Jesus answered that spirit in the opposite direction and said:

"*I say not unto thee, Until seven times: but, Until seventy times seven.*" (Matthew 18:22, KJV)

Because He forgave you, He commands you to forgive them.

That command is not cruelty.

It is rescue.

Forgiveness does not excuse evil.

It breaks evil's right to keep governing your soul.

"*And be ye kind one to another, tenderhearted, forgiving one another, even as God for Christ's sake hath forgiven you.*" (Ephesians 4:32, KJV)

Tenderhearted.

That is what forgiveness starts restoring.

What You Release to God Stops Governing You

Whatever you keep clutching keeps ruling.

Whatever you release to God stops governing you.

Some people are still being ruled by the same old wound because they still protect it as private property. They revisit it. They rehearse it. They identify by it. They draw energy from it. Then they wonder why the atmosphere stays heavy, why worship stays distant, why joy stays weak, why relationships stay strained, and why perception keeps going sideways.

It still governs because it was never released.

And this is where some people need to move quickly. Some need to write the note. Some need to make the call. Some need to clear the matter. Some need to get this mess right with family, with church people, with people who are still sitting in the soul like unpaid debt.

Not because the offense was small.

Because the soul is too expensive to lose.

What you release to God stops narrating reality for you.

What you hand over stops steering your perception.

What you surrender stops freezing your tenderness.

That is why forgiveness restores feeling.

It returns life to places bitterness had put on ice.

It returns perception where offense had clouded it.

It returns sensitivity where accusation had deadened it.

It returns the ability to feel God rightly again.

Forgiveness Is a Weapon

Forgiveness is not weakness. Asking forgiveness is not weakness. They are weapons.

Most people do not see it that way. Flesh thinks forgiveness is losing. Flesh thinks asking forgiveness is humiliation. Flesh wants retribution. Flesh wants to see somebody hurt long enough to feel justified. That spirit is not just in the world. It is all through the church. Some sinners forgive faster than Christians do. That should terrify you.

Jesus left no loopholes. *"Forgive every one"* (Luke 11:4, KJV). *"If ye have ought against any"* (Mark 11:25, KJV). *"If ye forgive not… neither will your Father forgive"* (Matthew 6:15, KJV). *"If ye from your hearts forgive not every one"* (Matthew 18:35, KJV).

From your heart.

Not from your mouth only. Not from your church face. Not from your religious vocabulary. From your heart.

So forgive all means all. Fathers, mothers, pastors, spouses, betrayers, church people, the one who lied on you, used you, wounded you, shamed you, disappointed you. And if forgive all means all, then all includes you too.

If you have repented and come under the blood of Jesus Christ, stop making yourself the one exception to mercy. *"If we confess our sins, he is faithful and just to forgive us"* (1 John 1:9, KJV). *"There is therefore now no condemnation"* (Romans 8:1, KJV). *"Their sins and iniquities will I remember no more"* (Hebrews 10:17, KJV). If God released you, stop keeping yourself chained.

Now hear this hard: if you will not forgive, you will not be forgiven.

That is not poetry. That is a sentence from Christ. So what did you think that meant? What did you think standing unforgiven before God meant? What did you think not entering the Kingdom meant? Do not play dumb with Jesus. If you refuse forgiveness and cling to offense, you are stepping into the fast lane to hell with church clothes on.

And asking forgiveness is a weapon too.

Do not use fake apologies, manipulative apologies, half apologies, or theater apologies. That is not righteousness. That is witchcraft in church language. But if you go quickly, humble yourself quickly, ask forgiveness quickly, and mean it in your heart, then you have obeyed God. You brought the matter into the light. You opened the sealed room. You moved the issue under the government of Christ.

Now the stumbling block is no longer in front of you. It is in front of them.

That is where Balaam comes in. Balaam was not a fool. He knew he could not curse what God had blessed, so he gave counsel that put a stumbling block in front of Israel (Numbers 31:16; Revelation 2:14). But Israel still sinned on their own. They could have refused. They chose sin, and the consequences were massive.

That still works.

If Satan cannot destroy you directly, he will try to get you through offense. If he cannot win through what was done to you, he will try to win through what you refuse to release. So be wise.

Forgive quickly. Ask forgiveness quickly. Mean it in your heart. Do not leave the breach sitting there. Do not let pride delay obedience.

Because once you obey, the stumbling block moves.

Now the other person has a choice. They can forgive and stay clean, or they can harden and step into danger. When you ask forgiveness and mean it, you have done in principle what Balaam did to Israel: you moved the stumbling block in front of them. If they refuse to forgive the right way, if they keep their poison, pride, and sin, they are the one choosing the stumbling block. They could have obeyed Christ. If they do not, the consequences are massive.

If they refuse real forgiveness and keep bitterness alive, they are no longer fighting you. They are fighting God. They are the one inviting chastening. *"Lest any root of bitterness… trouble you, and thereby many be defiled"* (Hebrews 12:15, KJV).

That is why forgiveness is a weapon. You obey fast. You get clean fast. You move the case into God's court fast.

And do not try to hide behind giving.

Jesus said if you bring your gift to the altar and remember your brother has ought against you, leave the gift there, go first, be reconciled, and then come back and offer it (Matthew 5:23-24). First. Not later. First.

That means you do not get to tithe over disobedience. You do not get to sing over bitterness. You do not get to serve over unforgiveness. God is not for sale. You cannot bribe heaven with an offering while refusing to obey Christ. God rejects sacrifice when the heart stays crooked (Isaiah 1:11-17; Proverbs 21:27). The fire will test every work anyway (1 Corinthians 3:13-15). So do not comfort yourself with, "Well, I still tithe." If your heart is poisoned with unforgiveness, your money does not impress God. It increases your accountability.

You can fake people. You cannot fake God.

So stop delaying. Stop bargaining. Stop calling your offense discernment. Stop calling your hardness wisdom. Stop calling your delay maturity.

Your greatest unknown weapon is this: ask forgiveness fast, and forgive fast, even when you were the one done wrong. Do it from the heart, do it in truth, and do it before pride talks you out of obedience. Because the moment you obey Christ, the first stumbling block moves out of your path and lands in theirs. If they refuse to forgive, refuse to reconcile, keep their sin, pride, and religious games, then they are no longer fighting you. They are fighting God. Their gift is corrupt. Their tithe does not impress God. Their volunteering does not impress God. Their ministry labor does not impress God. Works done with a poisoned heart will not stand the fire; they will be burned up at judgment (1 Corinthians 3:13-15). And if they think they can bypass Christ's command, ignore the person, and just "talk to God" while staying in disobedience, they are deceiving themselves, because Jesus said if you do not forgive, you will not be forgiven (Matthew 6:14-15; Matthew 18:35; Mark 11:25). Pride will destroy them, because God resists the proud (James 4:6), and the Lord chastens His own (Hebrews 12:5-11).

Now hear the other side clearly: forgiveness does not mean stupidity, and mercy does not mean giving evil unlimited access to your life. It is perfectly biblical to step back from angry, manipulative, divisive people. That is not bitterness. That is wisdom. *"Make no friendship with an angry man"* (Proverbs 22:24-25, KJV). *"Mark them… and avoid them"* (Romans 16:17, KJV). *"A man that is an heretick… reject"* (Titus 3:10, KJV). *"From such turn away"* (2 Timothy 3:5, KJV). *"Withdraw yourselves from every brother that walketh disorderly"* (2 Thessalonians 3:6, KJV). *"Evil communications corrupt good manners"* (1 Corinthians 15:33, KJV).

So yes, if a person is angry, manipulative, full of strife, or constantly sowing division, you do not owe them unlimited access to your life. And a title does not sanctify sin. If they are a church leader and still traffic in strife, control, division, flattery, intimidation, and manipulation, avoid them anyway. The Bible does not tell you to keep giving them access because they have a title; it tells you to mark them and avoid them.

Forgiveness is a weapon. Asking forgiveness is a weapon.

And when you use it quickly, truthfully, and from the heart, the devil loses one of his favorite doors. The wound no longer rules you. The poison no longer sits on the throne. The stumbling block is no longer in your path. Now the other person has to decide whether they will obey Christ or choke on their own bitterness.

That is hard. That is raw. That is ruthless. And that is exactly why it works. I will end with this last warning: You might think you got away with your bad attitude, pride, lies, unforgiveness and manipulation, and even got protected on earth by people or even church leaders. But it will be publicly seen by all at the throne in the end, and you will see things burned up before your eyes because you refuse to hear, see, and obey while living on earth.

Conclusion: Forgiveness Thaws What Bitterness Froze

The soul cannot heal while holding debt.

It cannot carry the flow of God cleanly while still hosting a private courtroom. It cannot stay open to mercy while preserving bitterness. It cannot walk in freedom while guarding offense like treasure. What you keep preserving keeps ruling. What you keep defending keeps poisoning. What you refuse to release keeps speaking inside you long after the event is over.

That is why unforgiveness is so deadly.

It does not only remember pain.

It protects poison.

It does not only revisit injury.

It keeps the soul tied to it.

It keeps the inward man shut when God is trying to open it.

So do not delay what Jesus told you to do.

Obey Christ fast.

Forgive fast.

Ask for forgiveness fast.

Make the call fast.

Write the note fast.

Go to the person fast.

Do not let pride buy one more day.

Do not let offense talk you into delay.

Do not let religion teach you how to disobey with spiritual language.

Because delay is not neutral.

Delay feeds bitterness.

Delay hardens pride.

Delay deepens deception.

Delay keeps the stumbling block alive.

Delay gives hell more room.

Delay keeps the soul shut when God is trying to open it.

So obey fast or pay for delay.

There is no reward for dragging your feet in disobedience. There is no blessing on spiritual excuses. There is no safety in pretending you can bypass the Word and still have peace. Christ already spoke. Forgive. Reconcile. Get it right. And if you obey, the matter moves into God's court. If the other person refuses, let God deal with them. But do not sit there and rot in the same poison while calling it discernment.

The soul heals in the light, not in delay.
The conscience clears in truth, not in bargaining.
Mercy moves fastest in the life that stops arguing with God.

Obey Christ fast: forgive fast and ask for forgiveness fast, or get run over by the consequences of your own pride. Hell loves delayed obedience because delayed obedience is still disobedience, and your own pride will become the shovel that digs your grave.

Scripture Index:

- Luke 11:4
- Matthew 6:14-15
- Matthew 13:15
- Matthew 18:21-35
- Matthew 18:22
- Romans 12:1
- Romans 14:17
- Ephesians 4:32
- Hebrews 3:13
- Hebrews 12:15
- Psalm 23:3
- Psalm 51:10
- James 1:22
- Genesis 4:24
- Luke 11:4
- Mark 11:25
- Matthew 5:23-24
- Matthew 6:15
- Matthew 18:35
- 1 John 1:9
- Romans 8:1
- Psalm 103:12
- Hebrews 10:17
- Numbers 31:16

- Revelation 2:14
- Hebrews 12:15
- Isaiah 1:11-17
- Proverbs 21:27
- 1 Corinthians 3:13-15
- James 4:6
- Hebrews 12:5-11
- Proverbs 22:24-25
- Romans 16:17
- Titus 3:10
- 2 Timothy 3:5
- 2 Thessalonians 3:6
- 1 Corinthians 15:33

Part IV

Back Under Design

You do not get whole by inventing a self. You get whole by coming back under the design of God. These chapters deal with the Logos, with sanity under truth, with daily bread, with false interpretation, and with the restoration of right order in thought, appetite, identity, and response. This is where contradiction is judged. This is where rival systems lose authority. This is where the false voices that trained the soul get confronted by the written Word of God. The issue is not self-expression. The issue is reality. When life comes back under the design that made it, peace stops being theory and begins becoming order.

"And be not conformed to this world: but be ye transformed by the renewing of your mind, that ye may prove what is that good, and acceptable, and perfect, will of God." (Romans 12:2, KJV)

Chapter Ten

Out of Your Design, Out of Your Mind

Introduction: Life Breaks When It Leaves Its Blueprint

Life does not break at random.

It breaks when it leaves its blueprint.

Much of what people call pressure is really contradiction with reality. Much of what they call mystery is misalignment. They are trying to live outside the order that made them, then acting shocked when the soul starts coming apart. They want identity without design, desire without government, freedom without obedience, peace without truth, and blessing without inward order. But the soul was never built to invent itself.

God made man with design, measure, order, and meaning. That means there is a rightness to life. There is a divine arrangement to thought, desire, sexuality, value, identity, relationship, worship, conscience, personality, and inward government. When that arrangement is violated, fracture enters the soul. It may not show up publicly on day one. A person can still smile, still function, still attend church, still work, and still look stable. But contradiction has entered the structure, and contradiction always sends a bill.

That is why some people look normal while thinking crooked, reacting crooked, loving crooked, choosing crooked, and building crooked. They did not merely make a mistake. They stepped outside design. And once life leaves design, the soul begins losing its mind one compromise at a time.

Design Is Not a Suggestion

God's design is not advice.

It is not a recommendation for unusually serious Christians. It is the architecture of reality. The Word of God is not one viewpoint among many. It is the fixed measure by which every other viewpoint is judged.

"For the word of God is quick, and powerful, and sharper than any twoedged sword, piercing even to the dividing asunder of soul and spirit..." (Hebrews 4:12, KJV)

The Word does not merely comfort.

It cuts.

It divides.

It tells you where your feelings ended and your rebellion began. It tells you where appetite disguised itself as identity, where fear disguised itself as wisdom, where damage disguised itself as personality, and where self-will learned how to use spiritual language. It tells you where reasoning drifted out of line with heaven.

That is why design feels hard to a rebellious soul. It exposes what the soul was trying to protect. It calls normal what culture calls extreme. It calls disorder what men have learned to call authenticity. It calls crooked what the age has renamed personal truth. And because the Word is true, it does not bend to preserve illusion.

The devil always wants to make what God says is reasonable seem unreasonable (Romans 12:1-2).

But heaven is not unreasonable.

Rebellion is.

God is not trying to shrink your life.

He is trying to stop you from destroying yourself while calling it self-expression.

To Live Against the Logos Is to Live Against Reality

To live against the Logos is to live against reality itself.

If Christ is the Logos, then He is not merely Savior. He is the operating principle behind life. He is the governing order. He is the design beneath design. And if all things were made by Him, then all things only make sense under Him.

"In the beginning was the Word, and the Word was with God, and the Word was God." (John 1:1, KJV)

"All things were made by him; and without him was not any thing made that was made. In him was life; and the life was the light of men." (John 1:3-4, KJV)

The world has order because it came from Him. Life has meaning because it came through Him. Sanity exists where things remain under His arrangement.

The moment you separate life from the Logos, you do not become more free.

You become more confused.

That is why private interpretation is so dangerous. People know what God has said, but they want to customize reality around appetite, wounds, pride, lust, culture, and preference. Then they play the God card. They call contradiction revelation. They call self-will discernment. They call deviation depth.

No.

What God is saying will never contradict what God has said.

If it contradicts the Logos, it is not revelation.

It is deception wearing church language.

This age keeps preaching shame-free rebellion. No shame for fornication. No shame for perversion. No shame for abortion. No shame for living against design. But the removal of shame does not remove consequence. Culture can normalize violation all day long, but normalization does not cancel structure.

You do not break the Logos.

The Logos breaks you.

You cannot go against the design inside of you without consequences. You cannot live against reality and stay sane. You cannot force life to run backward and keep peace in the inward man. Heaven does not adjust itself because rebellion had strong feelings.

Reality does not negotiate with rebellion.

Double-Minded Living Produces Inner Fracture

A double-minded man is not simply indecisive.

He is split in government.

"A double minded man is unstable in all his ways." (James 1:8, KJV)

There are people trying to hold two opposing ideas on the same subject in the same soul. They want God and self-rule. They want truth and private exemption. They want holiness and appetite. They want surrender and control. They want the blessing of the Logos while still reserving the right to edit the pattern.

That is not depth.

That is fracture.

You only get one mind.

You only get one will.

You only get one emotional center.

You only get one inward government.

Two opposing ideas on the same subject in the same inward man do not make you profound. They make you unstable. When one part of you says yes to truth while another part keeps protecting the lie, instability is not mysterious. It is the consequence of divided allegiance. Fog is not always complexity. Sometimes it is contradiction.

That is why some people have a church self, a private self, a business self, a sexual self, an angry self, and a religious self. They call it complexity. Heaven calls it division. The soul was never built to carry two masters in the same room. So the mind gets foggy, the emotions get erratic, the will gets compromised, and the conscience starts malfunctioning.

A divided man cannot stay clear.

A divided man cannot stay steady.

A divided man cannot stay whole.

Division in the soul always becomes disorder in the life.

Feelings Do Not Override Design

Feelings are real.

They are just not sovereign.

A generation has been trained to treat feelings like final authority. If they feel it strongly enough, it must be true. If they desire it deeply enough, it must be lawful. If the urge is loud enough, it must be identity. But a feeling can be sincere and still be wrong. A desire can be intense and still be disordered. An appetite can be loud and still need a cross.

Design does not bow to sensation.

Truth does not move because emotion was urgent.

God did not give you feeling so feeling could become your god. He gave you feeling so feeling could come under government. He gave you appetite so appetite could be glorified, not demonized. He gave you desire so desire could answer to the King. If feeling outranks Scripture, the soul will drift. If appetite outranks design, the life will bend. If desire outranks truth, the inward man will eventually call darkness light and bondage liberty.

That road does not end in freedom.

It ends in fracture.

What feelings refuse to surrender, they eventually use to rule.

"I beseech you therefore, brethren, by the mercies of God, that ye present your bodies a living sacrifice, holy, acceptable unto God, which is your reasonable service. And be not conformed to this world: but be ye transformed by the renewing of your mind..." (Romans 12:1-2, KJV)

Reasonable service.

Not unreasonable service.

God's pattern is not madness.

It is sanity.

Disorder in Life Begins with Disorder in Alignment

If you do not have the Logos in your life, you will measure by the wrong system.

You will interpret value through the lust of the flesh, the lust of the eyes, and the pride of life (1 John 2:15-17). You will decide worth by what can be displayed, worn, shown, envied, posted, purchased, or admired. That is the world's insanity.

A man does not need a thirty-thousand-dollar watch to tell time.

He needs it to tell a story.

Ask me what time it is.

Look at me.

Measure me.

Approve me.

That is the pride of life.

A house stops being shelter and becomes a monument. Possessions stop being useful and become identity props. A little logo on a shirt becomes a counterfeit sacrament. A new phone becomes a fresh hit of meaning until the next version comes out. Then the substitute fails, and the chase begins again.

The devil will keep you addicted to substitutes until you find the Logos.

Once measurement goes wrong, desire goes wrong.

When desire goes wrong, choices go wrong.

When choices go wrong, life starts breaking.

The soul cannot stay sane while worshiping symbols.

What you use to measure yourself will eventually master you.

"Love not the world, neither the things that are in the world... For all that is in the world, the lust of the flesh, and the lust of the eyes, and the pride of life, is not of the Father..." (1 John 2:15-16, KJV)

Sanity Returns When Life Comes Back Under Truth

The world is full of operating systems. Business system. Social system. Sexual system. Cultural system. Trend system. Status system. Family system. Church system. Every one of them is trying to tell you who you are, what matters, how to measure, and what success looks like. And if the Logos is not governing you, those systems will start redefining you.

They get into a thing, then the thing gets into them.

What began as participation becomes identity.

What began as environment becomes definition.

What began as influence becomes interpretation.

That is how people lose themselves without noticing.

Many people are not meeting the real you. They are meeting the version of you that has been bent by damage, trained by contradiction, and stabilized by wrong measurement. They are interacting with your soul damage, not your restored self.

Some have been so marked by bad fathers, dictators, manipulators, gossipers, drunkards, abusers, and crooked church cultures that they no longer let their personality express itself the way God designed it. They choke down lawful courage. They suppress clean joy. They hide clean strength. They flatten honest expression. Then they call that mutilation maturity.

No.

Damage taught them how to disappear.

Others have suffered so deeply that the soul no longer knows how to receive remedy. There are people who endured sexual abuse, occult corruption, betrayal by fathers, betrayal by leaders, and violations that should never happen. Then truth comes, prayer comes, help comes, correction comes, and the inward man cannot receive it cleanly because the damage has sealed the place where the remedy must go.

There is no place to put the remedy in a soul determined to protect its distortion.

That is why some people cannot receive clean truth, clean love, or clean correction. Everything gets misread. Order feels controlling. Holiness feels extreme. Strong preaching feels abusive. Normal relationships feel threatening. Why? Because the soul has lived in contradiction so long that disorder now feels normal and normal feels offensive.

Do crazy people know they are crazy?

No.

That is the problem.

Distortion feels normal from inside distortion.

Some people have even cut themselves just to feel something, because contradiction, trauma, and numbness shut down the inward life so badly that pain feels like proof of existence. That is what hell does. It drives a soul so far out of design that it starts using destruction to confirm that it is still alive.

But adaptation is not healing.

Familiarity is not wholeness.

Repetition is not righteousness.

When the Logos comes in, He does not cooperate with the counterfeit version. He rearranges everything on the inside. He steps into chaos and starts restoring structure. He restores right measurement. He restores sane interpretation. He restores lawful personality. He restores what damage twisted. He restores what religion suffocated. He restores what hell tried to redefine.

The Renewed Mind Returns the Soul to Sanity

"And be not conformed to this world: but be ye transformed by the renewing of your mind..." (Romans 12:2, KJV)

The renewed mind is not merely more informed.

It is reordered.

It stops letting feeling outrank Scripture. It stops letting culture outrank design. It stops letting damage define what normal is. It starts agreeing with God. Then the fog begins lifting. Private interpretation starts losing power. Status symbols stop mattering so much. Distortion gets named. The soul begins coming back into its right mind.

That is where peace begins.

Not in self-invention.

Not in emotional indulgence.

Not in customizing truth until it leaves you alone.

Peace begins where life comes back under the Logos.

"Casting down imaginations, and every high thing that exalteth itself against the knowledge of God, and bringing into captivity every thought to the obedience of Christ;" (2 Corinthians 10:5, KJV)

That is not behavior polish.

That is government.

That is the mind being taken back from contradiction.

Conclusion: You Cannot Live Whole While Resisting the Way You Were Made

You cannot stay whole while fighting the pattern that made you.

You cannot violate design and keep peace.

You cannot enthrone feeling above truth and keep sanity.

You cannot live in contradiction with reality and call the fracture complicated.

You cannot let the world's systems rename you and still expect your soul to stay whole.

You cannot keep measuring by pride of life and still know what anything is worth.

You cannot live off private interpretation and remain stable.

And you cannot keep suppressing what God lawfully designed in you, then wonder why the soul feels shut down, warped, or split.

The answer is not a softer lie.

The answer is surrender.

Come back under the Logos.

Come back under the Word.

Come back under the design that made life work.

Stop calling contradiction complexity.

Stop calling instability personality.

Stop calling pride-of-life measurement wisdom.

Stop calling deception depth.

Stop asking heaven to bless what reality itself rejects.

Because the soul does not become whole by demanding exemption from truth.

It becomes whole when truth is allowed to put everything back where it belongs.

And that is Kingdom normal.

Scripture Index:

- John 1:1-4
- Romans 7:14
- Romans 8:7
- Romans 12:1-2
- 2 Corinthians 10:5
- Hebrews 4:12
- James 1:8
- 1 John 2:15-17
- Proverbs 14:12
- Isaiah 55:8-9
- Psalm 119:105

Chapter Eleven

The Logos Restores Order

Introduction: Chaos Is Not a Personality Trait

Chaos is not a personality trait.

It is not depth.

It is not originality.

It is not mystery.

Most of the time, chaos is the evidence of something living outside the order that was meant to govern it. That is true in homes. It is true in churches. It is true in nations. And it is true in the soul.

The soul was not made to invent its own operating system. It was made to live under the Logos. The Word of God is not merely a collection of verses for comfort, inspiration, or occasional correction. It is the written expression of divine order. It is the fixed architecture of reality. It is heaven's operating system revealed in language. And when the soul lives outside that written order, confusion multiplies, contradiction deepens, and damage starts talking like wisdom.

That is why some people stay spiritually active while remaining inwardly unstable. They can move, serve, attend, quote, sing, preach, react, and still carry so much inner confusion that what should flow cleanly through them keeps coming out distorted. The issue is not always lack of sincerity. Many times the issue is that the soul is running on a false operating system.

God did not design you for internal contradiction.

He designed you for order.

He designed you for truth.

He designed you for reality under Christ.

Christ Is the Logos, Not Merely a Concept

Christ is not one truth among many.

He is the Logos.

That means He is not only the Savior who rescues you from sin. He is the governing Word through whom all things were made, the architecture beneath existence, the ordering intelligence of reality, and the standard by which all other claims must be judged.

"In the beginning was the Word, and the Word was with God, and the Word was God." (John 1:1, KJV)

"All things were made by him; and without him was not any thing made that was made." (John 1:3, KJV)

"And the Word was made flesh, and dwelt among us..." (John 1:14, KJV)

If all things were made through Him, then all things only make sense under Him.

That means Christ is not an accessory to life.

He is the explanation of life.

He is not a religious add-on to your already self-defined existence.

He is the center from which existence gets its meaning.

And when people try to live without the Logos governing them, they do not become free.

They become disordered.

The Word does not merely tell you how to survive.

It tells you what is real.

That is why every false system eventually crashes. It may run for a while. It may look impressive for a while. It may even feel empowering for a while. But if it is not aligned with the Logos, it is only borrowed momentum on the way to breakdown.

The Written Word Is Heaven's Operating System

The written Word of God is not decorative.

It is operational.

It does not exist merely to give the Christian inspiring lines to quote. It exists to bring the inward man under heaven's order. It reveals what is lawful, what is crooked, what is flesh, what is spirit, what is clean, what is corrupted, what is life-giving, what is destructive, what is wisdom, and what only sounds wise to a soul already bent by damage.

"For the word of God is quick, and powerful, and sharper than any twoedged sword, piercing even to the dividing asunder of soul and spirit..." (Hebrews 4:12, KJV)

That means the Word is not only comforting material.

It is dividing material.

It separates what you blended.

It exposes what you mislabeled.

It tells you where emotion was pretending to be discernment, where appetite was pretending to be identity, where fear was pretending to be caution, where pride was pretending to be strength, and where private preference was pretending to be revelation.

"And there is no creature that is not manifest in his sight: but all things are naked and opened..." (Hebrews 4:13, KJV)

The Logos does not cooperate with illusion.

It does not flatter your excuses.

It does not bend to your wounds.

It does not change because your feelings were intense.

It reveals reality and then summons the soul to come back under it.

That is why the written Word is so threatening to false operating systems. It keeps naming things correctly. It keeps confronting the private arrangement. It keeps exposing where the inward life has been organized around something other than Christ.

False Operating Systems Produce False Lives

Every false operating system eventually produces a false life.

If the soul is being governed by lust, fear, bitterness, victimhood, envy, pride, status, performance, religious tradition, emotional reasoning, or cultural propaganda, then life will be interpreted through that system. The person may still use Christian language, but the underlying arrangement is still wrong.

That is why some people keep getting the wrong outcome with the right vocabulary.

They keep saying "God," but they are operating out of fear.

They keep saying "discernment," but they are operating out of suspicion.

They keep saying "wisdom," but they are operating out of damage.

They keep saying "freedom," but they are operating out of rebellion.

They keep saying "peace," but they are operating out of numbness.

That is not a language problem.

That is an operating-system problem.

False Operating System vs. Logos Order

The soul becomes stable when it comes back under the architecture of truth.

JOHN 1:1
JOHN 17:17
COLOSSIANS 2:8
EPHESIANS 4:20-24

"There is a way which seemeth right unto a man, but the end thereof are the ways of death." (Proverbs 14:12, KJV)

A false system often feels right from the inside.

That is what makes it dangerous.

It can feel normal.

It can feel justified.

It can feel deep.

It can feel personal.

It can feel self-protective.

It can feel spiritually sophisticated.

But if it is not aligned with the Logos, it is still false.

And false systems produce false readings, false loyalties, false reactions, false measurements, and eventually false lives.

The Mind Justifies What the Heart Has Chosen

One of the clearest signs that a false operating system is running is this:

The mind starts defending what the heart had already chosen.

The person does not start with clean reasoning.

They start with disordered affection, hidden preference, appetite, offense, fear, pride, or private rebellion. Then the mind gets recruited to build arguments for the thing the soul already wanted.

That is why private interpretation is so dangerous.

A person can know what God has said, but because the heart has already chosen a contradiction, the mind starts customizing reality to make the contradiction feel lawful.

That is how men start saying:

- God told me.

- I have peace.

- This is just how I am.

- This is my truth.

- I do not see it that way.

- I think God is doing a new thing.

But what God is saying will never contradict what God has said.

If it contradicts the written Word, it is not revelation.

It is rebellion with spiritual language.

"Casting down imaginations, and every high thing that exalteth itself against the knowledge of God..." (2 Corinthians 10:5, KJV)

That verse matters because imaginations do not only mean fantasy.

They include internal thought-structures, mental arguments, self-protective reasonings, and exalted ideas that have lifted themselves above what God has already made plain.

The renewed mind tears those structures down.

It does not decorate them.

Split Government Produces Instability

You cannot run two operating systems in the same soul without instability.

You cannot enthrone Christ in language while enthroning self in practice and expect peace to remain. You cannot say yes to truth in public while building private exemptions in secret and expect the inward man to stay clear.

"A double minded man is unstable in all his ways." (James 1:8, KJV)

Double-mindedness is not just indecision.

It is divided government.

It is the soul trying to preserve two rival arrangements at once.

Truth says one thing.

Appetite says another.

The written Word says one thing.

The emotional demand says another.

Christ says one thing.

The false system says another.

That produces fog.

That produces fracture.

That produces instability.

The soul was never built to carry rival thrones.

That is why people can become so inwardly noisy. They are trying to live under contradictory commands. One part of them wants the peace of Christ. Another part wants the freedom to disobey without consequence. One part wants holiness. Another part wants exemption. One part wants healing. Another part still wants the wound to stay useful.

That is not complexity.

That is divided rule.

And divided rule always becomes disorder in life.

The Logos Rearranges Chaos from the Inside

When the Logos really enters a life, He does not merely add inspiration.

He rearranges chaos.

That is one of the strongest hopes in this whole chapter. Christ does not enter the inward life to admire the disorder. He does not step into confusion to politely coexist with it. He enters to reorder what has been thrown out of rank.

He rearranges affections.

He rearranges thoughts.

He rearranges loyalties.

He rearranges measurements.

He rearranges desires.

He rearranges what damage twisted.

He rearranges what fear froze.

He rearranges what false religion suffocated.

He rearranges what hell tried to redefine.

That is why some people can come from terrible homes, crooked authority, manipulation, abandonment, abuse, and years of contradiction, and yet become sane in Christ. The past may have taught the soul one pattern, but the Logos can step into that chaos and begin restoring heaven's pattern from the inside.

"And be not conformed to this world: but be ye transformed by the renewing of your mind..." (Romans 12:2, KJV)

Transformation is not decorative change.

It is reordering under truth.

That is why the renewed mind matters so much. It is not merely more informed. It is more governed. It stops letting culture, appetite, fear, and damage define what normal is. It begins agreeing with the Logos. Then peace returns because reality is no longer being resisted at the deepest level.

Religious Systems Can Also Be False Systems

Not every false operating system is secular.

Some are religious.

A person can be deeply shaped by tradition, performance culture, fear-based church structures, false holiness standards, suppression, control, and religious image management, and still call the result maturity. They may not look worldly, but the inward operating system is still crooked.

That is why religious souls can be some of the hardest to restore. They do not merely have wounds. They have theological language wrapped around the wounds. They do not merely have false measurements. They have Bible-sounding explanations for the false measurements.

But the Logos still cuts through that too.

He reveals where religion crucified what He meant to sanctify.

He reveals where fear got baptized as holiness.

He reveals where suppression got renamed maturity.

He reveals where a lawful personality got buried alive under somebody else's broken system.

That is why the Word must be allowed to operate cleanly.

Not as a slogan.

Not as a charm.

Not as a cultural prop.

As the governing standard of reality.

Order Returns Peace to the Soul

Peace is not mostly the reward of comfort.

Peace is the fruit of alignment.

When the inward life comes back under the Logos, noise begins losing power. Contradiction starts getting exposed. The false system starts collapsing. The soul no longer has to keep defending what reality itself rejects. The internal courtroom loses momentum. The self-justifying arguments begin drying up. The person does not become less intense because they got softer. They become less divided because they came back under order.

"Thou wilt keep him in perfect peace, whose mind is stayed on thee..." (Isaiah 26:3, KJV)

Perfect peace is tied to a governed mind.

Not a scattered one.

Not a self-arguing one.

Not a split-government one.

Not a privately customized one.

A mind stayed on God is a mind under order.

That is why the Logos restores peace.

He restores reality first.

Then the soul stops fighting what is real.

Conclusion: Come Back Under the Logos

The answer to inward confusion is not a softer lie.

It is not better branding for contradiction.

It is not more room for private interpretation.

It is not the freedom to keep running a false operating system while asking God for clean outcomes.

The answer is to come back under the Logos.

Come back under the written Word.

Come back under heaven's arrangement.

Come back under the fixed architecture of reality.

Let the Word tell you what is true.

Let the Word tell you what is disorder.

Let the Word tell you what is flesh.

Let the Word tell you what is spirit.

Let the Word tell you what was damage and what was design.

Let the Word expose the false system.

Let the Word dismantle the rival throne.

Let the Word reorganize the inward life.

Because the soul does not become whole by inventing itself.

It becomes whole when reality is allowed to put everything back where it belongs.

And that is what the Logos does.

Scripture Index:

- John 1:1-4
- Proverbs 14:12
- Isaiah 26:3
- Romans 12:2
- 2 Corinthians 10:5
- Hebrews 4:12-13
- James 1:8
- Colossians 1:16-17
- Psalm 119:89
- Psalm 119:105
- 1 Corinthians 14:33
- Ephesians 4:23

Chapter Twelve

Daily Bread for a Restored Mind

Introduction: Maintenance Is Not Optional

A beginning is not a maintenance plan.

A new car may come off the lot with a full tank, but nobody with sense believes that one tank was meant to carry the vehicle for life. When that fuel runs out, maintenance is no longer a theory. It becomes a requirement. You must do something. You must refill what was designed to keep receiving supply. That is not failure. That is design.

The soul works the same way.

Many people want one encounter to do what only daily bread can do. They want one altar, one service, one impartation, one emotional breakthrough, one prophetic moment, one season of unusual help to carry them for the rest of their lives. But God did not design the inward man to live on yesterday's fuel. He did not save you and then leave you to survive on memory. He did not put you in a crooked world and expect your mind to remain sound without supply. He did not call you to walk through the cosmos with no maintenance plan for the soul.

"But he answered and said, It is written, Man shall not live by bread alone, but by every word that proceedeth out of the mouth of God." (Matthew 4:4, KJV)

If man must live by every word, then maintenance is not optional.

It is built into the design.

You do not stay clear by accident. You do not stay ordered by accident. You do not stay spiritually sane by accident. If the soul is not being fed, it is being weakened. If it is being weakened, it is becoming unstable. And if it is becoming unstable, eventually the animal nature, the damaged reactions, the old appetites, the crooked interpretations, and the unhealed places will begin answering life for you again.

That is why daily bread is not religious routine.

It is the maintenance plan for a restored mind.

Daily Bread Is How the Soul Stays Aligned

Every living thing must be fed.

That is not poetry. That is law.

If it lives, it feeds. If it stops feeding, it weakens. If it weakens, it misfires. If it misfires long enough, something else starts taking over. That is why many people who love God still live unstable in practical ways. It is not always because they hate God. It is often because they are underfed.

"Give us this day our daily bread." (Matthew 6:11, KJV)

That prayer is not sentimental. It is severe. It is an admission that I was never meant to walk into today on yesterday's crumbs. It is a confession that every day has its own collisions, temptations, opportunities, lies, pressures, relationships, blind spots, and crazy people. You will meet crazy every day. You will meet pressure every day. You will meet yourself every day. Therefore God wants to feed you before you walk into the day that will test you.

Daily bread is preemptive mercy.

He feeds you before the collision.

He feeds you before the decision.

He feeds you before the temptation.

He feeds you before the conversation.

He feeds you before the wilderness starts talking.

That is why a neglected Word life is not a small omission. It leaves the soul trying to answer a loaded day without fresh alignment. Then people wonder why they keep making dumb decisions, wrong alliances, impulsive responses, emotional agreements, and costly mistakes. But God was never asking you to improvise your life. He was offering daily bread because He knew you would need daily alignment.

You cannot function effectively in the world system without a word from God.

Not just as a Christian.

As a human being.

"Thy word have I hid in mine heart, that I might not sin against thee." (Psalm 119:11, KJV)

"Thy word is a lamp unto my feet, and a light unto my path."
(Psalm 119:105, KJV)

If the Word is not hidden in the heart, the heart starts hiding from the Word.

Presence Without Word Produces Instability

Some people want presence without Word.

They want a touch without a training. They want a moment without a structure. They want fire without government. They want visitation without formation. They want power without the written order that keeps power from being mishandled. But presence without Word produces instability.

You can speak in tongues and still have a wrecked soul.

You can cry in a service and still think crooked.

You can feel God deeply and still answer life through damage the next morning.

Why? Because not everything spiritual is automatically soul restoration. Some things come out of your spirit. But your soul still has to be restored, renewed, trained, washed, separated, and reordered by the written Word of God.

That is why some people have spiritual vocabulary without spiritual stability.

They know how to sound alive without knowing how to stay aligned.

They know how to react in a meeting without knowing how to respond in life.

They know how to feel God for a moment without knowing how to carry His order through Monday, conflict, money pressure, temptation, relationships, fatigue, and disappointment.

That is not maturity.

That is instability with a testimony.

"And be not conformed to this world: but be ye transformed by the renewing of your mind..." (Romans 12:2, KJV)

Renewing is not a one-time event.

Renewing is ongoing resistance against drift.

That is why one encounter does not remove the need for daily bread. One encounter may awaken you. It may expose you. It may help you. It may mark you. But the soul stays aligned through ongoing feeding. If you refuse that, eventually something else will start talking louder than truth. Mood will talk louder. Fear will talk louder. Appetite will talk louder. Culture will talk louder. Pain will talk louder. Offense will talk louder.

And once that happens, people stop answering life from Christ and start answering life from whatever they kept feeding.

You will be a failure without daily bread.

That line is hard because it is true.

The Written Word Separates Soul from Spirit

The written Word of God does not flatter mixture.

It separates.

"For the word of God is quick, and powerful, and sharper than any twoedged sword, piercing even to the dividing asunder of soul and spirit... And there is no creature that is not manifest in his sight: but all things are naked and opened unto the eyes of him with whom we have to do." (Hebrews 4:12-13, KJV)

That means the written Word is not merely inspirational material. It is a knife. It divides what you blended. It exposes what you mislabeled. It shows you what is spirit and what is soul, what is conviction and what is reaction, what is hunger and what is lust, what is wisdom and what is fear, what is discernment and what is suspicion, what is holiness and what is pride dressed in religious language.

Many people are restricted by their own affections (2 Corinthians 6:11-12). Their inward life is locked up by loves, fears, wounds, appetites, loyalties, opinions, and reactions they never brought under the knife of the Word. Then they call that inner restriction personality. They call it maturity. They call it caution. They call it "just how I am." But the Word exposes what your soul has been using to keep itself barricaded.

The mind justifies what the heart has chosen.

That is why some people fight the written Word while pretending they are just being thoughtful. No. They have chosen something in the heart, and now the mind is working overtime to defend it. Science says. The culture says. Big Mama says. The court says. My feelings say. My history says. My wound says. My preference says. And all the while the written Word is standing there like a plumb line, refusing to move.

The Holy Spirit does not bypass the Logos.

He manifests it.

He takes what God has said and makes it alive in you. He makes it real in you. He makes it confront you, cleanse you, nourish you, and reorder you. But He does not make you whole by helping you neglect the book already in your hands.

Those little inspirational crumbs stuck on the refrigerator are not daily bread.

That is a Christian fortune cookie.

Bible roulette is not discipleship.

"All scripture is given by inspiration of God, and is profitable... That the man of God may be perfect, throughly furnished unto all good works." (2 Timothy 3:16-17, KJV)

Scripture Reorders Thought, Desire, and Response

The soul does not stay ordered because you are sincere.

It stays ordered because it is governed.

Scripture reorders thought by confronting lies. It reorders desire by exposing false love. It reorders response by slowing the soul down long enough to answer from truth instead of bruise, impulse, or appetite. It reorders the inward arrangement of things.

*"If ye then be risen with Christ, seek those things which are above...
Set your affection on things above, not on things on the earth."* (Colossians
3:1-2, KJV)

Affection is not a decorative word.

Affection governs direction.

What you love will steer you. What you crave will interpret
life for you. What you secretly prize will begin editing your
theology, your relationships, your reasoning, your standards, and
even your prayers. That is why Scripture does not merely inform
the mind. It reorders affection. It retrains desire. It brings loves
back into rank.

A broken soul justifies what it has already chosen.

That is why some people can hear truth for years and still
stay crooked in the same areas. Their problem is not lack of
exposure only. Their problem is disordered affection. The soul has
already voted, and the mind keeps writing speeches to defend the
decision.

But Scripture will not cooperate with that.

It keeps pressing.

It keeps cutting.

It keeps calling things by their right names.

It keeps saying, "This belongs above. This belongs below.
This is clean. This is crooked. This is spirit. This is flesh. This is
order. This is confusion. This is Christ. This is self."

That is mercy.

Because until your inward arrangement changes, your outward life will keep leaking confusion.

"Wherewithal shall a young man cleanse his way? by taking heed thereto according to thy word." (Psalm 119:9, KJV)

Sheep Eat Slow: Why Repetition Matters

Many people despise repetition because they mistake recognition for possession.

They hear a truth once, nod at it, quote it, and assume they own it. They do not. Recognition is not digestion. Agreement is not embodiment. Hearing is not incorporation. Sheep eat slow.

That is why God gave four Gospels telling the same Christ from multiple angles. Sheep are ruminants. Sheep have four sections in their stomach. When they eat something initially, they take in a mouthful of grass or grain, and it goes into the first chamber. There it begins to be broken down. Then they bring it back up and chew it again. Then it is distributed into the second chamber. They repeat that process into the third chamber, and by the fourth chamber it goes out. That is how sheep eat. They do not swallow once and call it done. They work it through again and again until it has fully moved through them.

That is why God put basically the same story in four different Gospels. Sheep eat slow.

Repetition is not divine redundancy.

It is mercy for slow creatures.

Sheep eat slow.

That line is not an insult. It is an explanation.

People come to church, do not read the Word of God, and then everybody assumes they understand what is being said. They do not. Some are intelligent but ignorant. They have the capacity, but they have not been exposed enough, chewed enough, processed enough, or fed enough for the thing to actually live in them. So they nod in church-polite agreement while the truth still has not landed deeply enough to order the soul.

That is why repetition matters.

That is why the same truths must be preached again.

That is why the same Scriptures must be revisited again.

That is why the same Christ must be shown again.

Not because heaven is empty of content, but because sheep eat slow.

Repetition is the mother of learning.

The soul often does not break in one hearing. It often yields under repeated exposure. Truth comes once and informs. Truth comes again and presses. Truth comes again and starts exposing resistance. Truth comes again and begins to dislodge what has been defending itself for years. That is how digestion works.

Some people are not rebellious in every area.

They are just under-chewed.

"As newborn babes, desire the sincere milk of the word, that ye may grow thereby." (1 Peter 2:2, KJV)

Growth is tied to intake.

A Neglected Word Life Produces a Confused Inner Life

If you are not reading the Bible, you had better check and see if you are alive.

That line is hard, but it exposes something real. Every living thing must be fed. If you are not feeding on daily bread, then what part of you are people mostly meeting? Too often, they are meeting your animal nature, your unrenewed reactions, your damaged reasoning, your unwashed preferences, your inherited distortion, your emotional weather, your defensive reflexes, your old programming.

That is why a fish on the back of the car proves nothing.

External markers are cheap.

A Christian bumper sticker is cheap.

Religious language is cheap.

Public identity is cheap.

If the soul is not being fed, under pressure what comes out will tell the truth.

A neglected Word life produces a confused inner life. Thought gets foggy. Affection gets misplaced. Judgment gets cloudy. Reaction gets unreliable. People begin calling bondage freedom, appetite identity, preference discernment, and damage wisdom. They can still attend, still sing, still serve, still say the right phrases, and still be inwardly unstable because the mind is not under sufficient renewal to stay sane.

A person can become less sane without becoming less religious.

That is the terror.

God never designed your life to run on random inspiration, weak fragments, or occasional borrowed feeding. He meant for you to open the book, ask the Holy Spirit to make the written Word alive, and stay there until the soul comes back under government.

Read your Bible until the Word starts reading you.

Read your Bible until your excuses lose oxygen.

Read your Bible until the mind stops justifying what the heart had chosen.

Read your Bible until the inner noise starts bowing.

Read your Bible until the animal nature stops being the first thing people meet.

"This book of the law shall not depart out of thy mouth; but thou shalt meditate therein day and night..." (Joshua 1:8, KJV)

Meditation is not passivity.

It is repeated inward processing until the Word governs response.

Conclusion: A Soul Fed Daily Does Not Stay Mentally Broken

A soul fed daily does not stay mentally broken.

It may begin damaged. It may begin bruised. It may begin reactive, foggy, defensive, lustful, proud, fearful, unstable, restricted by its own affections, and mixed up between soul and spirit. But if it is fed daily, it does not stay that way. The Word keeps cutting. The Word keeps washing. The Word keeps separating. The Word keeps reordering. The Word keeps exposing. The Word keeps making the inward life answer to reality again.

That is why daily bread is not optional.

It is not a hobby for intense Christians.

It is not a luxury for leaders.

It is not a private preference.

It is maintenance for sanity.

If you neglect it, do not be shocked when more beast than Christ comes out of you in traffic, conflict, money pressure, temptation, fatigue, disappointment, and offense. Do not be shocked when what people mostly meet is your damage, your instability, your appetite, or your unrenewed reactions. Do not be shocked when you keep circling the same confusions and calling them mysterious. Underfed souls become confused souls.

But there is a remedy.

Go to the Bible.

Go to the Bible and say, "Holy Spirit, make the written Word alive in my heart. Make it alive in my spirit. Make it something I can feel, taste, and touch. Feed me before I walk into this day. Give me the word I need for my family, my decisions, my finances, my relationships, my wilderness, my blind spots, my future."

Come back to the Logos daily.

Come back hungry.

Come back teachable.

Come back slow enough to digest.

Because the soul that is fed daily does not stay dull.

The soul that is fed daily does not stay unstable.

The soul that is fed daily does not stay mentally broken.

It comes back under order.

It comes back under truth.

It comes back under the mind of Christ.

And when the inward man is fed rightly, life stops being interpreted by damage and starts answering to the Word of God.

"Then said Jesus to those Jews which believed on him, If ye continue in my word, then are ye my disciples indeed; And ye shall know the truth, and the truth shall make you free." (John 8:31-32, KJV)

Scripture Index:

- Matthew 4:4
- Matthew 6:11
- John 8:31-32
- Romans 12:2

- 2 Corinthians 6:11-12
- Colossians 3:1-3
- 2 Timothy 3:16-17
- Hebrews 4:12-13
- James 1:21
- Joshua 1:8
- Psalm 119:9
- Psalm 119:11
- Psalm 119:105
- 1 Peter 2:2

Part V

The Soul Made Whole

The goal is not merely that the pain quiets down. The goal is that the soul becomes whole. This final movement gathers the burden of the book into restoration, identity, purpose, usefulness, and government. Here the reader is brought toward healed naming, recovered design, restored feeling, and the condition of a soul that can finally carry truth, light, life, and weight without collapsing or turning muddy on the way through. This is where relief yields to wholeness. This is where damage stops narrating the future. This is where the inward man comes back under the hand of the Shepherd and becomes fit for the life God meant to flow through it.

"He restoreth my soul: he leadeth me in the paths of righteousness for his name's sake." (Psalm 23:3, KJV)

Chapter Thirteen

Restored Sight

Introduction: If Sight Is Damaged, Life Gets Misread

If sight is damaged, life gets misread.

Not only natural sight.

Soul sight.

Spiritual perception.

Inward interpretation.

The ability to recognize what is from God, what is from the flesh, what is clean, what is mixed, what is true, what is counterfeit, what is mercy, what is temptation, what is wisdom, and what is merely something your damaged soul wanted to call good.

That is why restored sight matters.

A person can be sincere and still see crooked.

A person can love God and still misread life.

A person can have zeal and still have disordered affection.

A person can want the Kingdom and still keep choosing substitutes because the soul has not learned how to see cleanly.

That is where so much bondage survives.

Not only in appetite.

In perception.

Because if you do not see rightly, you will not choose rightly. If you do not discern rightly, you will attach wrongly. If you cannot tell the difference between what is alive and what only imitates life, you will keep making agreements that wound the soul while telling yourself you are walking in wisdom.

Everything that comes to you in the spirit requires perception before reception.

If perception is damaged, reception is damaged too.

That is why this chapter is not merely about information.

It is about sight.

The Soul Can Learn to Live by Substitutes

One of the most dangerous things a damaged soul can do is learn how to live by substitutes.

A substitute is something you let stand in the place of what God actually intended.

A substitute is not always obviously evil at first glance. That is why it is dangerous. It can look useful, comforting, spiritual, sophisticated, compassionate, practical, modern, balanced, or even wise. But if it takes the place of what God actually said, what God actually designed, what God actually ordered, then it is still a substitute.

And substitutes wound people because they keep the soul from getting the real thing.

A substitute can stand in the place of truth.

A substitute can stand in the place of love.

A substitute can stand in the place of conviction.

A substitute can stand in the place of holiness.

A substitute can stand in the place of communion.

A substitute can stand in the place of the Word.

A substitute can stand in the place of the real Christ while still using His language.

That is why damaged sight is so costly. If you do not see clearly, you will keep bonding to replacements.

"Woe unto them that call evil good, and good evil; that put darkness for light, and light for darkness..." (Isaiah 5:20, KJV)

That verse is not just about public wickedness.

It is about corrupted sight.

It is about the inward confusion that starts calling the wrong thing right.

Ordered Affection Determines Clear Sight

You do not only see through your mind.

You see through your loves.

Affection is not decorative.

Affection is interpretive.

What you love starts steering what you call wise. What you crave begins shaping what you call necessary. What you secretly want begins editing what you are willing to see, what you are unwilling to confront, and what you are prepared to excuse.

That is why the soul must not only be informed.

It must be reordered.

"If ye then be risen with Christ, seek those things which are above... Set your affection on things above, not on things on the earth." (Colossians 3:1-2, KJV)

If affection is set wrongly, sight will be bent.

If affection is set rightly, discernment starts clearing up.

That is why some people can read the same Scripture and come away with different conclusions. One soul is looking for surrender. Another soul is looking for permission. One soul is looking for light. Another soul is seeking a substitute that will let self stay enthroned.

The mind justifies what the heart has already chosen.

So if the heart is disordered, vision follows it into confusion.

A Damaged Soul Misreads What It Sees

The soul does not merely receive life.

It interprets life.

That is why damaged sight is so destructive.

A bruised soul can misread kindness as threat.

A fearful soul can misread caution as wisdom.

A proud soul can misread correction as insult.

A lustful soul can misread bondage as identity.

A religious soul can misread life as disorder.

A wounded soul can misread ordinary love as intrusion.

A dull soul can misread strong truth as abuse.

That is why the issue is not always whether truth is present.

The issue is whether the soul can still see it cleanly.

"Having the understanding darkened, being alienated from the life of God through the ignorance that is in them, because of the blindness of their heart:" (Ephesians 4:18, KJV)

Blindness of heart is not poetic language.

It is diagnostic language.

It means the problem is not only out there.

It is in the inward man.

And if the inward man is darkened, then even when truth is close, the person experiences it as distant, threatening, confusing, or severe.

That is why a restored soul is not a luxury.

It is the condition required for healthier sight.

Everything in the Spirit Requires Perception Before Reception

This is one of the governing lines for the whole chapter.

Everything that comes to you in the spirit requires perception before reception.

If you do not perceive it, you will not receive it properly.

If your eyes are closed to it, the benefit may be present and still not become yours.

A healing can be in the room and still be missed.

A word can be in the room and still be missed.

A warning can be in the room and still be missed.

A mercy can be in the room and still be missed.

A visitation can be in the room and still be misread.

That is why perception matters so much.

You can still be going to heaven and yet take the rocky road to get there because your perception has been dulled.

That is not because God withheld good.

It is because damaged sight kept misreading what was available.

"The light of the body is the eye: if therefore thine eye be single, thy whole body shall be full of light. But if thine eye be evil, thy whole body shall be full of darkness..." (Matthew 6:22-23, KJV)

Christ did not say sight was a side issue.

He tied it to the whole condition of the person.

Substitutes Feel Easier Than the Real Thing

One reason substitutes are so dangerous is that they often feel easier than the real thing.

A substitute asks less surrender.

A substitute asks less repentance.

A substitute asks less patience.

A substitute asks less discipline.

A substitute asks less dying.

A substitute lets the soul keep some of its idols while still pretending to move toward God.

That is why the soul keeps reaching for them.

A person can sing instead of obeying.

A person can perform instead of changing.

A person can repeat language instead of cultivating truth.

A person can gather information instead of receiving light.

A person can seek relief instead of receiving restoration.

A person can seek admiration instead of holiness.

A person can seek charisma instead of Christ.

That is not harmless.

That is substitution.

"Little children, keep yourselves from idols." (1 John 5:21, KJV)

Idols are not only statues.

Anything that takes the place of what God actually intended is functioning as an idol.

Discernment Is Not Suspicion

Discernment is one of the first casualties when sight is damaged.

Then people start calling suspicion discernment.

They call negativity discernment.

They call preference discernment.

They call offense discernment.

They call fear discernment.

They call old wounds discernment.

But discernment is not your damage getting a microphone.

Discernment is not the soul reacting from bruising.

Discernment is clean sight under the rule of truth.

"But strong meat belongeth to them that are of full age, even those who by reason of use have their senses exercised to discern both good and evil." (Hebrews 5:14, KJV)

That verse matters because it ties discernment to exercised senses.

Not flattered senses.

Not indulged senses.

Not suspicious senses.

Exercised senses.

That means discernment is strengthened through maturity, repetition, use, submission, and the training of the inward man under the Word of God.

A damaged soul will call many things discernment that are actually fear, envy, pride, or projection.

That is why this chapter cannot stop at "see better."

It must press further.

Your senses must be exercised under truth until the soul stops misnaming what it carries.

Restored Sight Comes Through the Word

Sight is not restored by wishing.

It is restored by light.

It is restored by truth.

It is restored by the Logos.

If the soul is bent, the Word confronts the bend.

If affection is disordered, the Word calls it back into rank.

If substitutes have been enthroned, the Word pulls the false thing down.

If the soul keeps trying to call evil good and good evil, the Word refuses to cooperate.

"Thy word is a lamp unto my feet, and a light unto my path." (Psalm 119:105, KJV)

"The entrance of thy words giveth light; it giveth understanding unto the simple." (Psalm 119:130, KJV)

That means understanding is not magic.

It comes through light entering.

And when light enters, confusion gets contradicted.

That is why the person who stays away from the Word should not be surprised when substitutes feel convincing. Without light, replacements become persuasive. Without light, disorder looks normal. Without light, affection remains misarranged. Without light, the soul keeps arguing for what is killing it.

Healed Sight Produces Different Walking

When sight is healed, walking changes.

That is the evidence.

A person with healed sight does not only talk better.

They walk differently.

They attach differently.

They choose differently.

They respond differently.

They refuse things they once excused.

They recognize things they once missed.

They recoil from things they once tolerated.

They stop making peace with the substitutes that once fed their damage.

That is why healed sight matters so much.

Because eventually sight becomes direction.

"I will instruct thee and teach thee in the way which thou shalt go: I will guide thee with mine eye." (Psalm 32:8, KJV)

God does not only want to rescue you from blindness.

He wants to guide you through restored sight.

And when the soul sees better, affection orders better.

When affection orders better, discernment functions better.

When discernment functions better, walking changes.

Conclusion: Ask God to Heal Your Sight

This chapter is not a call to become clever.

It is a call to become clear.

Ask God to heal your sight.

Ask Him to expose your substitutes.

Ask Him to reorder your affection.

Ask Him to show you where your soul has been defending what it should have rejected.

Ask Him where you have been calling something wisdom that was only damage with better language.

Ask Him where your loves have been steering your sight.

Ask Him where the soul has been making agreements with replacements.

"Open thou mine eyes, that I may behold wondrous things out of thy law." (Psalm 119:18, KJV)

That is a good prayer for this whole chapter.

Open my eyes.

Not my excuses.

Not my preferences.

Not my substitute systems.

My eyes.

Because restored sight is mercy.

It is how the soul stops living by replacements and starts walking according to truth again.

It is how affection gets reordered.

It is how discernment gets cleaned up.

It is how the soul stops calling darkness light.

It is how the inward man starts walking according to healed sight.

Scripture Index:

- Isaiah 5:20
- Matthew 6:22-23
- Psalm 32:8
- Psalm 119:18
- Psalm 119:105
- Psalm 119:130

- Colossians 3:1-2
- Ephesians 4:18
- Hebrews 5:14
- 1 John 5:21
- 2 Corinthians 4:4
- Proverbs 4:23

Chapter Fourteen

Identity Restored, Purpose Recovered

Introduction: The Devil Attacks Identity First

The devil rarely begins by attacking your calendar.

He attacks your definition.

He does not start by fighting your schedule, your money, your geography, or your opportunities. He starts by fighting who you believe you are, what you believe you are worth, what you believe your life means, and whether you still believe God can build anything clean out of what you have been through. He knows that if identity goes crooked, choices go crooked. If choices go crooked, purpose starts dragging behind a wounded soul.

That is why hell strikes identity early.

It struck in Eden.

It struck in the wilderness.

It still strikes now.

"Now the serpent was more subtil than any beast of the field which the LORD God had made. And he said unto the woman, Yea, hath God said...?" (Genesis 3:1, KJV)

That was not merely a question about fruit.

It was an attack on definition, trust, and design. The enemy struck identity at the beginning by challenging what God had said and by seducing man to seek identity, wisdom, and elevation apart from obedient union with God.

"And when the tempter came to him, he said, If thou be the Son of God, command that these stones be made bread." (Matthew 4:3, KJV)

"If thou be the Son of God, cast thyself down..." (Matthew 4:6, KJV)

That was not merely temptation about bread or spectacle.

It was an assault on sonship, definition, and trust. The devil struck in the wilderness by attacking who Jesus was and by trying to separate power from obedience, identity from submission, and sonship from the written Word.

"Beloved, believe not every spirit, but try the spirits whether they are of God..." (1 John 4:1, KJV)

And it still strikes now. The battle is still over identity, over what God has said, over whether a person will live by divine definition or by deception, appetite, culture, wounds, and private interpretation.

"So God created man in his own image, in the image of God created he him." (Genesis 1:27, KJV)

Identity was never supposed to be invented from below.

It was supposed to be received from above.

The enemy knows that if he can detach the soul from God's definition, he can make a person spend years trying to build a self that never had grace on it.

The enemy wants the soul reading itself through shame, failure, comparison, appetite, status, rejection, and old damage instead of through the Word of God. Because once identity is damaged, people start answering life from distortion. They make bargains a whole soul would refuse. They cling to substitutes. They measure themselves by broken scales. They call confusion personality. They call pain maturity. They call limitation realism.

But the devil is not attacking you because you are worthless.

He is attacking you because identity governs movement.

"If thou be the Son of God..." (Matthew 4:3, KJV)

That was not a question about power.

That was a strike at definition.

And once definition is struck, direction becomes vulnerable.

Broken Identity Produces Broken Choices

Broken identity does not stay internal.

It starts making decisions.

If you do not know who you are in God, you will start borrowing identity from the material world. You will read meaning through labels, logos, applause, platforms, possessions, and social recognition. A stitched symbol on a shirt can start carrying more emotional weight than the Word of God. A brand name on a shoe, an emblem on a car, a title on a business card, or a little logo on a sleeve can start deciding whether you feel up or down that day. That is how low the soul can fall when identity is no longer anchored in Christ.

Some people get depressed because they do not have the little symbol.

They are reading value through the wrong logos.

That is not a small issue. That is a soul asking the material world to tell it what matters, what counts, what proves worth, and what signals arrival. But the material world cannot tell you who you are. It can only distract you while you forget.

A soul that does not know its identity will sell itself cheap.

It will mistake appetite for destiny.

It will mistake attention for affection.

It will mistake visibility for value.

It will mistake movement for purpose.

It will mistake being wanted for being called.

A wounded identity will eat what a whole identity would reject.

A damaged soul will call poison provision if it gets hungry enough.

That is why broken identity always produces broken choices. The inward man starts making decisions from lack instead of design. And once the soul starts answering from lack, it can call almost anything necessary. It can justify compromise. It can excuse disorder. It can embrace relationships, habits, ambitions, and definitions that do not fit the Kingdom, simply because the soul is starving for a name.

The Logos Rewrites the Story of the Soul

The answer to damaged identity is not self-esteem.

It is the Logos.

"In the beginning was the Word, and the Word was with God, and the Word was God." (John 1:1, KJV)

Jesus Christ is not an add-on to your already existing life. He is the architect of reality. He is not a religious accessory clipped onto your personality. He is the ordering principle of all things. He is the One by whom all things were made, held together, maintained, and carried toward their appointed purpose.

"All things were made by him; and without him was not any thing made that was made." (John 1:3, KJV)

"Who being the brightness of his glory, and the express image of his person, and upholding all things by the word of his power..." (Hebrews 1:3, KJV)

So when the Logos comes into a life, He does not merely comfort chaos.

He enters it and starts rearranging everything.

He rewrites value.

He rewrites meaning.

He rewrites order.

He rewrites purpose.

He rewrites what gets to stay.

That is why the Logos does not merely forgive you.

He reorganizes you.

The man from the dysfunctional family is not finished if the Logos enters.

The woman with the broken past is not finished if the Logos enters.

The life that started crooked is not finished if the Logos enters.

"Therefore if any man be in Christ, he is a new creature: old things are passed away; behold, all things are become new." (2 Corinthians 5:17, KJV)

That verse is not permission for denial.

It is permission for redefinition under Christ.

The past may explain what happened. It does not get final naming rights once the Logos enters.

The Logos comes into chaos and starts speaking structure where confusion used to rule. He enters distorted value systems and starts bringing everything back under true weight. He enters false meanings and starts stripping them of authority. He steps into the inward life and asks one severe question:

Who told you that this broken version of yourself was final?

The Logos does not consult your damage for permission to restore you.

He confronts what has been ruling you and starts bringing the soul back under truth.

He does not ask darkness for a testimony before He turns the light on.

Delay Is Not the Same as Denial

Many people think a delayed destiny is a dead destiny.

It is not.

Delay is not denial. Delay can be mercy. Delay can be formation. Delay can be protection from being crowned too early while the inward man is still misaligned.

Some of you have called God absent when He was actually being wise.

Some have called Him unfaithful when He was actually being merciful.

Some have called delay rejection when heaven was actually preventing ruin.

There are promises that become dangerous in the hands of the unformed. There are doors that become judgment if entered before the soul comes back under order. There are opportunities people beg for that would only magnify confusion if granted too soon.

So hear it clearly:

Delayed is not denied!!!

"For we are his workmanship, created in Christ Jesus unto good works, which God hath before ordained that we should walk in them." (Ephesians 2:10, KJV)

If the works were ordained before, then delay did not surprise God.

Your history may have tangled the road, but it did not erase the design.

The Logos can enter a damaged life, a drug-infested history, a teenage mistake, a family wreckage, a failed season, a hidden shame, and still bring purpose out of it. God is not intimidated by the chronology of your confusion. He is not trapped by how long it took you to get here. He is not standing in heaven wondering whether your history ruined His design.

No.

He is waiting for alignment.

He is waiting for surrender.

He is waiting for the soul to stop defining the future by the mess behind it.

Do not accuse God of denial when He is saving you from premature exposure.

You Must Stop Reading Life Through the Rear-View Mirror

You cannot drive into purpose while staring at what is behind you.

Some people are living their entire lives through the rear-view mirror. A past failure still interprets every current possibility. An old shame still narrates every present opportunity. A teenage mistake still gets final commentary over a grown life. An old addiction, an old accident, an old wound, an old betrayal, an old humiliation still keeps speaking as though Christ never entered the story.

That is captivity.

Not humility.

Captivity.

The rear-view mirror has a purpose, but it was never meant to be your windshield. It is useful for reference. It is disastrous for direction.

"...forgetting those things which are behind, and reaching forth unto those things which are before," (Philippians 3:13, KJV)

Some of you keep rereading your old chapter until you have mistaken it for your current identity. But when the Logos enters a life, He does not merely improve the old story. He starts rewriting the measure by which the story is read. He comes into the chaos. He comes into the lack of meaning. He comes into the confusion. He comes into the wreckage and starts rearranging the inward life around truth instead of trauma.

Quit living life in the rear-view mirror.

Quit treating old pain like present authority.

Quit giving old damage the right to name you.

Quit letting history do what only Christ is allowed to do.

The past may explain where you bled.

It does not get to prophesy where you end.

Purpose Is Found in Alignment, Not Ambition

Purpose is not found by chasing importance.

It is found by coming into alignment.

The world teaches ambition.

The Kingdom teaches alignment.

The world says invent yourself.

The Kingdom says submit yourself.

The world says build a name.

The Kingdom says receive one.

The world says chase prominence.

The Kingdom says follow the Logos until your life comes back under design.

You do not cruise into the will of God.

You set your face.

You pick up your cross.

You forsake all.

You follow.

"For the Lord GOD will help me; therefore shall I not be confounded: therefore have I set my face like a flint..." (Isaiah 50:7, KJV)

"Then said Jesus unto his disciples, If any man will come after me, let him deny himself, and take up his cross, and follow me." (Matthew 16:24, KJV)

That is not the language of spiritual tourism.

It is discipleship.

A great many believers want the promises without the alignment. They want acceleration without surrender. They want meaning without obedience. They want reward without the cross. But many New Testament promises are disciple promises. They belong to those who align themselves with the Word of God, not merely those who admire it from a distance.

Alignment is what gives ambition permission to die.

Alignment is what turns desire into destiny.

Alignment is what converts scattered energy into holy usefulness.

If you are out of alignment with the Logos, your life will keep feeling incomplete even when outward things are going well. You can have activity without meaning, motion without purpose, church without discipleship, attendance without transformation, and religion without inward order. But once the soul comes into alignment, purpose stops feeling vague. It starts becoming obvious.

Ambition wants a platform.

Alignment wants a cross.

Ambition wants to be seen.

Alignment wants to be true.

The Restored Soul Stops Living Beneath Its Calling

A restored soul does not keep introducing itself by its damage.

It stops living beneath its calling.

It does not keep saying, "This is just how I am," when what it really means is, "This is how I was wounded." It does not keep bowing to family dysfunction, old shame, cultural definitions, or false limitations. It does not keep confusing body trouble with spirit defeat.

There was a man in a wheelchair who said it plainly:

"My spirit is not sick. Just my body."

The body may be under pressure.

The history may be messy.

The timeline may have been delayed.

But the spirit does not have to stay misnamed.

That one statement exposes how many people have allowed natural pressure to rewrite spiritual identity. A limitation in the body is not permission for defeat in the spirit. A difficult history is not proof that purpose died. Circumstances can press the outer man without being granted authority to rename the inner man.

"And the angel of the LORD appeared unto him, and said unto him, The LORD is with thee, thou mighty man of valour." (Judges 6:12, KJV)

Gideon did not look like what heaven called him.

But heaven did not read him by his fear.

Heaven read him by his design.

God still does that.

He names according to purpose, not merely according to present condition.

A restored soul lets the Logos rearrange its value system until purpose becomes clearer than pain. It starts valuing people over things. It starts recognizing that significance is not measured by fame in the city but by faithfulness in the house. Some people may never be known in the newspaper, never trend in the culture, never have the platform the world admires, and still be deeply significant in the body of Christ because they carry prayer, care, truth, strength, service, supply, and quiet usefulness. Heaven does not measure importance the way the world does.

If you do not understand that, you will live for things and not for people.

You will live for image and not for impact.

You will live for possession and not for purpose.

God does not heal you to erase you.

He heals you to restore you.

He does not sanctify you by deleting lawful design. He sanctifies you by bringing lawful design under holy government. He does not flatten personhood. He cleanses it, orders it, and makes it usable. A healed identity stops begging to be seen and starts becoming fit to be sent.

From Audience to Army

God is not building an audience.

He is building an army.

An audience likes inspiration without surrender. An audience likes atmosphere without assignment. An audience likes feeling something as long as it is not required to become something. An audience likes being near the move of God as long as the move of God does not start disrupting convenience, exposing compromise, rearranging priorities, or demanding obedience. An audience enjoys sound. An army yields to command.

That is a dividing line.

An audience wants comfort.

An army accepts government.

An audience wants a touch.

An army accepts a commission.

An audience wants relief.

An army accepts responsibility.

That shift is not merely a maturity issue.

It is often an identity issue.

Damaged people spend most of their energy protecting themselves. They guard wounds, defend reactions, preserve excuses, and negotiate every demand. Restored people become available to heaven. A healed soul can say yes where a bruised soul keeps bargaining. A healed soul can receive command where a damaged soul only wants soothing.

God is not merely trying to produce people who attend.

He is raising people who obey.

He is not building a crowd that likes sermons. He is building a people who can carry weight, move under command, endure process, and remain steady while doing it. The restored person becomes useful because the inward life stops fighting the assignment. The restored person becomes useful because heaven can finally pour without everything turning muddy on the way through.

Conclusion: When Identity Is Healed, Destiny Can Move Again

When identity is healed, destiny stops dragging.

The devil attacks identity first because identity governs movement. If he can damage definition, he can delay purpose. If he can corrupt value, he can bend choices. If he can keep you reading life through old shame, old appetite, old comparison, and old pain, he can keep destiny stalled under a false name.

But the Logos rewrites the story of the soul.

He steps into chaos.

He steps into confusion.

He steps into damaged value systems.

He steps into lost years.

He steps into delayed lives.

He steps into the place where the wrong voice has been naming you.

So stop reading your future through your wound.

Stop reading your calling through your past.

Stop reading your value through the material world.

Stop calling delay denial.

Stop calling bondage personality.

Stop calling confusion identity.

Let the Logos enter.

Let the Logos rearrange.

Let the Logos rename what darkness tried to define.

Because once identity is healed, purpose is no longer foggy.

Once identity is healed, obedience stops feeling random.

Once identity is healed, destiny can move again.

The false name loses authority.

The inward man stands up clean.

And destiny stops limping.

Scripture Index:

- Genesis 1:27
- Genesis 3:1
- Matthew 4:3
- Matthew 4:6
- Matthew 16:24
- John 1:1-3
- 1 John 4:1

- Hebrews 1:3
- 2 Corinthians 5:17
- Ephesians 2:10
- Philippians 3:13
- Isaiah 50:7
- Judges 6:12

Chapter Fifteen

Soul Made Whole

Introduction: Restoration Is the Return of Government

Restoration is not relief.

Relief can lower the noise and reduce the sting for a moment, but relief is not wholeness, and quiet is not government. A soul can feel better for a week and still be ruled by fear. A soul can have a good service, a deep cry, a holy moment, and still go home governed by the same inward fracture that has been distorting life for years. Temporary calm is not the same thing as inward rule.

Restoration is the return of government.

It is the inward life brought back under the rule of God. It is the soul no longer steered by reaction, appetite, memory, old injury, private confusion, false comfort, or hidden disorder, but brought back under the hand of the Shepherd. It is when the mind stops wandering as an orphan, the emotions stop rioting as rebels, the will stops bargaining as a traitor, and the inward man comes back under the reign of Christ. Heaven is not merely after your confession. Heaven is after your condition. God is not content to save your spirit and leave your soul in pieces.

"And the very God of peace sanctify you wholly; and I pray God your whole spirit and soul and body be preserved blameless unto the coming of our Lord Jesus Christ." (1 Thessalonians 5:23, KJV)

God said wholly.

Not your spirit only.

Not your church life only.

Not your public language only.

Wholly.

Spirit, soul, and body.

That means God is not building patched people. He is restoring whole people. He is not applying religious paint to internal ruin or teaching damaged people how to perform spiritual language while their inward life still leaks disorder. He is restoring the whole man.

A saved spirit with an unruly soul is still a problem. A born-again person with a fractured inward life can still misread truth, poison relationships, mishandle weight, waste favor, resist correction, and flip ministry backward. The issue is not whether grace has touched them. The issue is whether the inward man has returned to government. Until government returns, damage keeps speaking. Until rule returns, reaction keeps interpreting. Until the soul comes under God, the old fracture keeps trying to narrate reality.

And damage is a terrible narrator.

Wholeness Is More Than Relief

Wholeness is more than symptom management.

It is more than finally getting a little peace. More than finally having fewer emotional crashes. More than learning how to control your tone in public. More than finding language to describe what hurts. More than becoming functional enough to survive church, family, leadership, responsibility, or memory. Wholeness is not managed fracture. Wholeness is healed order.

A soul can learn church language and still be broken. A soul can quote verses and still be disordered. A soul can shout, dance, cry, prophesy, serve, teach, and still drag private chains through every room it enters. Some people do not need a softer explanation. They need their inward life brought back under the government of Christ.

"He restoreth my soul: he leadeth me in the paths of righteousness for his name's sake." (Psalm 23:3, KJV)

Notice the order. He restores the soul, then He leads in paths of righteousness. Why? Because an unrestored soul cannot walk straight for long. It may visit righteousness, but it cannot sustain it. It may admire truth, but it cannot carry it. It may desire peace, but it still keeps leaning toward what wounded it. It may want freedom, but the inward life still answers to older masters.

Relief says, "I feel better right now."

Wholeness says, "My inward life is coming back under the King."

Relief quiets symptoms.

Wholeness changes rule.

Relief can make pain more manageable.

Wholeness makes the soul governable.

That is the difference.

Do not settle for relief and call it restoration. Do not confuse temporary quiet with inward order. Do not mistake an emotional exhale for full recovery. God did not come merely to reduce your discomfort. He came to reclaim your interior life. He came to bring the soul back from scattering, from confusion, from bondage, from false refuge, from old interpretation, and from the rule of inward chaos.

A soul is not whole because it has stopped screaming.

A soul is whole because it has come under God.

A Whole Soul Can Carry Light, Truth, and Weight

A damaged soul cannot carry weight cleanly.

It reacts to ordinary touch like a bruise reacts to a finger. A bruise may not be bleeding outwardly, but it is bleeding inwardly. Touch it normally and the response is abnormal. Press it lightly and the reaction is oversized. That is how many people live. They are bleeding beneath the surface, so normal correction feels like hatred, normal accountability feels like oppression, normal responsibility feels like punishment, and normal truth feels like danger. They are not reacting to what touched them now. They are reacting to what was already injured.

That is not discernment.

That is bruising.

A bruised soul misreads everything. It does not only feel pain. It manufactures distortion. It makes clean things seem hostile. It makes straight things seem cruel. It makes light seem invasive. It makes holy pressure seem unfair. It takes what was sent to heal and interprets it as something sent to destroy. That is one of the most destructive works of soul damage: it corrupts interpretation. It does not merely wound feeling. It bends perception.

"For the word of God is quick, and powerful, and sharper than any twoedged sword, piercing even to the dividing asunder of soul and spirit..." (Hebrews 4:12, KJV)

The Word separates what your damage keeps blending together. It exposes where reaction has been masquerading as discernment. It exposes where fear has been pretending to be wisdom. It exposes where pain has been speaking as though it were revelation. It exposes where the soul has been answering before the spirit even has a chance to speak. That is not cruelty. That is mercy. God is kind enough to divide what damage has confused.

"And there is no creature that is not manifest in his sight: but all things are naked and opened unto the eyes of him with whom we have to do." (Hebrews 4:13, KJV)

A whole soul can carry light, truth, and weight without calling them too bright, too sharp, or abusive.

A whole soul does not collapse every time reality presses on it. A whole soul can bear responsibility. A whole soul can receive correction. A whole soul can hold covenant. A whole soul can endure process. A whole soul can carry spiritual substance without demanding that everything be reduced to its present comfort level.

That is why inward healing matters so much.

A whole soul can carry what a damaged soul drops.

A whole soul can steward what a bruised soul reverses.

A whole soul can hold peace while carrying pressure.

The Restored Person Becomes Useful to Heaven Again

A restored soul becomes useful again.

Not dramatic.

Not theatrical.

Not merely expressive.

Useful.

That is restored identity talking. Wholeness does not deny bodily pressure. It refuses to let bodily pressure define the inward man.

There are gifted people heaven cannot trust with weight yet because their inward life keeps bending everything. They drag old injury into new assignments. They bring old suspicion into clean relationships. They import old fear into present opportunity. They love God, but their soul still has issues, and those issues keep turning favor backward. The problem is not always the lack of gift. Many times the problem is that the interior life is still too damaged to carry the gift cleanly.

A fractured soul cannot steward calling well.

A bent soul cannot carry ministry straight.

A leaking inward life keeps turning blessing backward.

There are born-again people going to heaven whose soul is still badly out of order. Their spirit belongs to Christ, but their mind, will, memory, emotions, conscience, and affections are still dragging yesterday's wreckage through today's assignment. So the inward life keeps sabotaging what grace is trying to build. They are not without a hope of salvation. They are without wholeness. And without wholeness, even real grace can get repeatedly mismanaged.

That is why restoration is not optional.

"Create in me a clean heart, O God; and renew a right spirit within me." (Psalm 51:10, KJV)

Some were not denied because God withheld from them. Some were delayed because their soul was still leaking. Some were not lacking opportunity. They were lacking inward healing. Some were not unusable because heaven had forgotten them. They were unusable because the inward life was still too injured to carry weight without distortion. Some are promoted by man, even in the midst of blatant Soul damage, because the promotion was not from God but from the will of man. A man who also had soul damage, and the opportunity was not in His will. And that promotion became a punishment to the people and the leader.

Then there is the matter of personhood.

If your personality is never sanctified, expressed, healed, and brought under truth, the person begins to disappear inside. If lawful personhood is constantly smothered, edited, intimidated, flattened, or controlled, the person becomes depressed. Not because God designed them for gloom, but because something He intended to bring into order was instead buried alive.

God does not heal you to erase you.

He heals you to restore you.

And heaven's measurements are not the city's measurements. Some people are never famous in the city, but they are deeply significant in the house. They carry prayer, steadiness, care, supply, truth, courage, and hidden strength. Restoration teaches the soul to stop chasing visibility and become fit for usefulness.

The Kingdom Flows Best Through a Healed Interior Life

The Kingdom flows best through a healed interior life.

That is not soft language.

That is spiritual mechanics.

"Keep thy heart with all diligence; for out of it are the issues of life." (Proverbs 4:23, KJV)

Not the issues of ministry only. Not the issues of prayer only. The issues of life. If the interior channel is inflamed, restricted, infected, bent, or cluttered, then what flows out will carry the inward disorder with it. You can have favor and still mistrust it. You can have love and still choke on it. You can have truth and still misread it. You can have calling and still sabotage it. Why? Because the soul keeps coloring everything that passes through it.

This is why healing matters. A healthy interior life stops inverting reality. It stops making every touch about the old wound. It stops turning clean leadership into threat, clean love into suspicion, clean process into oppression, and clean correction into humiliation. A healed soul no longer demands that everyone else tiptoe around what God is trying to restore.

And affection matters here more than many people understand.

Affection is not a small thing. Affection is directional power. Where you attach your inner love becomes a tow bar. It pulls you. It drags you. It moves you whether you meant to move or not. Whatever has your affection starts getting leverage over your direction. That is why disordered love is never innocent.

Wrong affection can tow an entire life into ruin. Right affection can pull the soul toward peace, clarity, obedience, stability, and joy.

"Delight thyself also in the LORD; and he shall give thee the desires of thine heart." (Psalm 37:4, KJV)

That is not indulgence language.

That is alignment language.

Delight changes desire.

Affection changes direction.

What you love starts teaching you where to go. If your inward life loves the wrong refuge, the soul keeps being dragged back into confusion. If your inward life delights in the Lord, the interior world begins to come into order, and the river of life starts flowing cleanly.

"Set your affection on things above, not on things on the earth." (Colossians 3:2, KJV)

The Kingdom does not flow best through a noisy interior life.

It flows best through a healed one.

From Audience to Army

God is not trying to build an audience.

He is building an army.

An audience likes inspiration without surrender. An audience likes atmosphere without assignment. An audience likes being near the move of God as long as the move of God does not start disrupting convenience, exposing compromise, rearranging priorities, or demanding obedience. An audience enjoys sound. An army yields to command.

That is a serious dividing line.

An audience wants comfort.

An army accepts government.

An audience wants a touch.

An army accepts a commission.

An audience wants relief.

An army accepts responsibility.

That shift is not merely a maturity issue. It is often a wholeness issue. Damaged people spend most of their energy protecting themselves. They guard wounds, defend reactions, preserve excuses, and negotiate every demand. Restored people become available to heaven. A healed soul can say yes where a bruised soul keeps bargaining. A healed soul can receive command where a damaged soul only wants soothing. A healed soul can carry burden without calling it cruelty.

"Thou therefore endure hardness, as a good soldier of Jesus Christ." (2 Timothy 2:3, KJV)

That is why wholeness matters to the Kingdom. God is not merely trying to produce people who attend. He is raising people who obey. He is not building a crowd that likes sermons. He is building a people who can carry weight, move under command, endure process, and remain steady while doing it.

The Good Shepherd Still Restores Souls

The Shepherd still restores souls.

He is not intimidated by deep damage. He is not confused by inward fracture. He is not exhausted by complexity. He is not put off by the things you hid, the reactions you normalized, the chains you decorated, or the private ruins you learned to manage. He knows exactly where the soul bent. He knows exactly where the bruise formed. He knows exactly where affection got chained to the wrong thing. He knows exactly where fear entered, where confusion settled, where memory took root, where false refuge formed, and where the inward life lost its government.

And He still comes.

"The thief cometh not, but for to steal, and to kill, and to destroy: I am come that they might have life, and that they might have it more abundantly." (John 10:10, KJV)

That is not survival language.

That is restoration language.

That is Shepherd language.

That is whole-life language.

The Road to a Soul Made Whole

The Shepherd restores the soul by bringing what is damaged into truth, renewal, and right response.

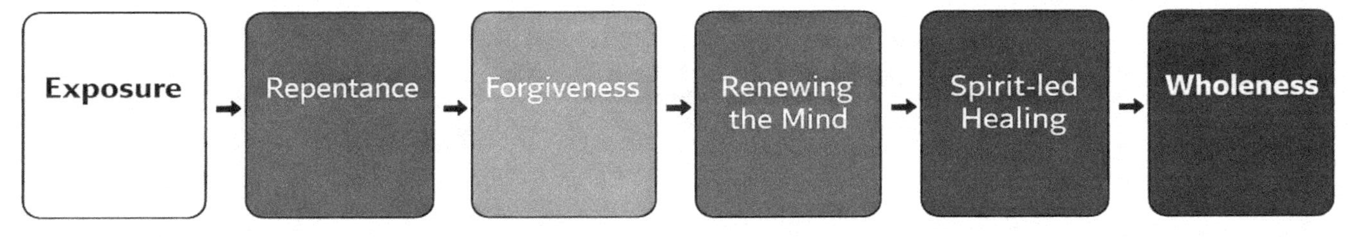

When wrong starts feeling normal, the soul has already been wounded.

Ps. 23:3 • Rom. 12:2 • John 7:38

He comes into the sanctuary of the Christian soul. He comes where the noise is. He comes where the fracture is. He comes where the inward life has been split, dulled, dragged, crowded, bruised, scattered, or disordered. And He is not coming merely to inspect the damage. He is coming to restore what was damaged, reorder what was disordered, and govern what has been left wild.

The Shepherd does not merely sympathize with brokenness.

He restores the soul.

Conclusion: What Hell Damaged, Christ Can Make Whole

Not prettier.

Not quieter only.

Not managed.

Not temporarily relieved.

Whole.

There is no new version of Jesus coming. You do not need an improved Christ. You do not need a softer gospel, a more flattering theology, or a more comfortable path. You need your soul brought under the One already enthroned. The answer is not a revised Savior. The answer is the government of God returning to the inward man.

The mind can be renewed.

The affections can be reordered.

The bruised places can stop ruling interpretation.

The inward life can stop flipping grace backward.

The damaged can become useful.

The scattered can become governed.

The fractured can become whole.

The audience can become an army.

So stop defending what God is trying to heal.

Stop naming damage personality.

Stop calling bondage normal.

Stop baptizing dysfunction as sensitivity.

Stop protecting the bruise that keeps corrupting your sight.

Stop mistaking relief for restoration.

Stop making peace with an inward life that still refuses government.

"And be not conformed to this world: but be ye transformed by the renewing of your mind." (Romans 12:2, KJV)

The Good Shepherd still restores souls.

And when He restores the soul, He does not merely make life easier. He makes the person usable. He puts clarity where there was distortion, rule where there was chaos, strength where there was weakness, peace where there was inward noise, and purpose where there was drift. He restores until the inward life can carry what heaven intended it to carry.

What hell damaged, Christ can make whole.

And a whole soul in the hands of God is a dangerous thing.

Scripture Index:

- Psalm 23:3
- Psalm 37:4
- Psalm 51:10
- Proverbs 4:23
- John 10:10
- Romans 12:2
- Hebrews 4:12-13
- Colossians 3:2)
- 2 Timothy 2:3
- 1 Thessalonians 5:23
- 2 Corinthians 6:11-12
- James 1:22

Glossary of Terms

Animal Nature

The flesh-driven part of man that resists the rule of God and pushes appetite, impulse, lust, fear, pride, and self-protection to the front. In this book, the animal nature is not the true ruler of life. It is the part that must be crucified so the spirit can lead and the soul can be restored.

Audience Christianity

A shallow form of church life where people want inspiration, atmosphere, and emotional benefit without surrender, obedience, discipleship, or transformation. In this book, the soul is not healed by staying an audience. God is forming an army, not a crowd.

Bitterness

Pain that has taken root and begun interpreting life. Bitterness does not merely remember injury. It keeps old injury alive, distorts relationships, warps judgment, and freezes tenderness until the soul can no longer feel or receive cleanly.

Bondage Management

The act of maintaining a damaged condition instead of confronting it for healing. In this book, bondage management may look polished, spiritual, quiet, mature, or controlled, but it is still bondage being preserved rather than broken.

Broken Choices

Decisions produced by damaged identity, disordered affection, dulled perception, or untreated wounds. In this book, broken choices are not random. They reveal the condition of the inward man making them.

Broken Identity

A condition in which the soul no longer reads itself through God's definition, but through shame, failure, comparison, rejection, appetite, status, or old damage. In this book, broken identity produces broken choices and delayed purpose.

Bruised Soul

A soul that reacts out of old injury instead of present truth. In this book, a bruised soul makes normal touch feel unbearable, normal correction feel hostile, and normal relationships feel threatening. A bruised place overreacts because it is still bleeding inside.

Captivity

A condition in which the soul is no longer reading life freely and cleanly through truth, but through damage, bondage, deception, or old wounds. In this book, captivity often sounds normal to the captive until Kingdom light reveals the chains.

Clean Feeling

Right inward response. Not sentimentality, but a restored capacity to answer God, truth, love, holiness, conviction, and correction without old poison hijacking the response.

Concealment

The act of hiding what needs to be brought into light. Concealment protects bondage, not healing. In this book, concealment is not wisdom or dignity. It is darkness defending its address.

Conviction

The work of God that exposes what is wrong so it can be healed, corrected, or surrendered. In this book, conviction is not cruelty. It is mercy. It is one of the signs the soul is still alive enough to respond rightly.

Counterfeit

A false substitute that imitates what only God can truly give. In this book, counterfeit relief, love, identity, peace, or spirituality become especially persuasive when the soul loses perception and starts hungering for life without recognizing the real thing.

Damage Has a Doorway

A governing phrase in the book, meaning soul damage, does not appear randomly. Something opened the way. Sin, shame, trauma, concealment, false religion, abuse, fear, or repeated compromise may become the doorway through which damage enters the inward life.

Dehumanized

A condition in which a person stops responding like a healthy image-bearer of God and begins adapting to darkness, injury, confusion, and captivity as though such conditions were normal. In this book, dehumanization strips tenderness, sobriety, clean perception, and holy reflex.

Delay Is Not Denial

A governing identity-and-purpose principle in the book. Delay may be mercy, formation, or protection, not abandonment. God may be preserving a person from being crowned too early while the inward man is still misaligned.

Desensitized

The condition of a soul that has lost its proper response. What should disturb no longer disturbs. What should convict no longer convicts. What should awaken grief or holy fear no longer penetrates. In this book, desensitization is not strength. It is injury left untreated long enough to impersonate stability.

Destiny

The God-ordained direction, usefulness, and purpose of a life under divine order. In this book, destiny does not move cleanly when identity is damaged, perception is

dulled, or the soul is ruled by the past. When identity is
healed, destiny can move again.

Discernment

The God-given ability to read what is true, false, clean,
mixed, holy, or crooked. In this book, discernment is not
suspicion, offense, negativity, or soul bruising with a
microphone. Discernment requires a healed interior life
and exercised senses.

Divided Government

An inward condition in which the soul tries to preserve
rival arrangements at the same time. Truth says one thing,
appetite says another. In this book, divided government
produces instability, fog, fracture, and loss of peace.

False Operating System

Any internal or external governing pattern that teaches a
person to think, feel, judge, choose, or interpret life apart
from the Logos of God. In this book, culture, fear, lust,
shame, pride, false religion, and humanism can all function
as false operating systems.

Favor Without Alignment

A false expectation that blessing can be enjoyed while the
soul remains out of order, resistant, concealed, or
disobedient. In this book, benefit is often lost not because
God stopped giving, but because perception and alignment
were lost.

Forgiveness

The releasing of debt so the soul can thaw, tenderness can return, and perception can live again. In this book, forgiveness is not pretending evil was small. It is refusing to stay chained to it.

Glossary of the Soul

The core vocabulary through which this book teaches inner-life restoration. Terms are not decorative. They are diagnostic and prophetic. They expose what damages the soul, what blocks the flow of God, and how restoration returns the inward man to order.

He Cannot Restore What You Won't Reveal

A governing principle of the book. God works in light. If the wound stays sealed, healing stays random. If the truth stays edited, the soul stays untreated. Restoration requires unveiled agreement with God.

Hidden Wounds

Soul injuries that remain unseen in explanation but not in effect. In this book, hidden wounds still speak through anger, withdrawal, lust, defensiveness, sarcasm, fear, or collapse, even when the person cannot clearly explain why.

Identity

The God-defined meaning of who a person is, what they are worth, and what their life is for. In this book, identity must be received from above, not constructed from damage, appetite, culture, or comparison.

Identity Restored

The recovery of God's definition over a life after false names, shame, failure, and distortion have ruled. In this book, restored identity makes purpose clearer than pain and usefulness clearer than self-protection.

Inner Refrigeration

A phrase describing what unforgiveness does to the soul. It freezes tenderness, trust, worship, openness, and courage, leaving the inward life cold while pretending the coldness is wisdom.

Kingdom Normal

God's definition of what is healthy, holy, sane, clean, ordered, and rightly responsive. In this book, Kingdom normal is not measured by damaged culture, repeated dysfunction, or what a wounded generation can tolerate. It is measured by God.

Logos

The written and governing Word of God, and in its highest sense Christ Himself as the ordering principle of reality. In this book, the Logos is not merely information. It is divine architecture, the maintenance system of life, and the standard by which all private interpretations, desires, and cultural systems must be judged.

Managed Self

The edited public version of a person that remains presentable while the real wound stays hidden. In this book, God is not healing the managed self. He is after the real man and the real woman.

Mercy

God's movement toward the damaged, exposed, guilty, or bound in order to restore, forgive, and heal. In this book, mercy does not protect concealment. It opens what secrecy buried so healing can begin.

Mystery Is in Your Sin History

A key phrase meaning the history of sin, damage, compromise, shame, trauma, and soul injury often explains the present condition of the inward man. In this book, identifying the history helps identify the wound so healing stops being random.

Perception

The inward ability to recognize, interpret, and identify what God is doing, what truth is present, and what should be received. In this book, perception is essential to spiritual life. When perception is damaged, reception is damaged.

Perception Before Reception

A central law of the book. Everything that comes in the spirit must first be perceived before it can be properly received. If the soul loses perception, it loses benefit, even when truth, help, healing, or presence are near.

Private Courtroom

An inward condition in which the soul keeps replaying old cases, holding debt, preserving accusations, and demanding payment from those who wounded it. In this book, the private courtroom blocks forgiveness, freezes feeling, and keeps the inward man from returning to life.

Private Interpretation

The attempt to customize reality around appetite, wounds, culture, pride, or preference while still using God-language. In this book, what God is saying never contradicts what God has said. Private interpretation becomes deception when it departs from the Logos.

Purpose

The God-ordained meaning, function, and usefulness of a life under divine order. In this book, purpose is not found by chasing importance, but by coming into alignment with the Logos.

Random Medicine

A book image for generalized ministry applied to unnamed wounds. When people hide the real issue, counsel becomes guesswork, pressure becomes misplaced, and help stays broad instead of targeted. In this book, healing stops being random when truth is told.

Rear-View Mirror Living

A way of living in which the past keeps narrating the present and defining the future. In this book, old failure, shame, or damage must not become the windshield through which destiny is read.

Relief

Temporary easing of pressure, pain, or noise. In this book, relief is not the same as restoration. Relief may calm symptoms, but only restoration returns the inward life to government and order.

Remedy

The healing, truth, and divine intervention God intends to put into the damaged place. In this book, there is no place to put the remedy until the soul opens.

Restoration

The work of God in healing, reordering, cleansing, and recovering what damage, sin, bitterness, or deception distorted. In this book, restoration is not cosmetic. It is the return of right order, right response, and right government.

Restored Feeling

The return of right inward response. Not sentimentality, but clean tenderness toward God, truth, holiness, worship, correction, and love. In this book, forgiveness and healing restore feeling by thawing what bitterness, shame, and damage froze.

Shame

The dark force that teaches the soul to hide, edit, shrink, distort, or remain inaccessible. In this book, shame does not merely make a person feel bad. It helps keep the soul concealed from truth and remedy.

Soul

The inward life through which a person thinks, chooses, feels, remembers, imagines, responds, and interprets life. In this book, the soul is the main battlefield of damage and restoration. A born-again spirit does not remove the need for soul healing.

Soul Damage

The injury left in the inward life by sin, trauma, shame, false religion, concealment, abuse, fear, bitterness, or repeated disorder. In this book, soul damage is not condemnation language. It is diagnosis language.

Soul Restoration

The work of God in healing, reordering, cleansing, and restoring the inward man. In this book, soul restoration is more than relief. It is the return of right response, right perception, right feeling, and right government under the Shepherd.

Spiritual Flow

The life of God moving through a person. In this book, even when life originates in the spirit, it must flow through the soul in lived experience. That is why soul condition matters so much.

Spiritual Refrigeration

A vivid phrase for what unforgiveness does to the inner life. It freezes tenderness, trust, openness, courage, and worship, leaving the soul cold while pretending the coldness is wisdom.

Split Government

A condition in which the soul tries to preserve two rival arrangements at once. In this book, split government produces instability, contradiction, and inner fracture.

Substitutes

False replacements accepted in place of what God actually intended. In this book, the damaged soul often bonds to substitutes when it loses the ability to perceive and receive the real thing.

The Kingdom Must Flow Through Your Soul

The life of God may originate in the spirit, but in lived experience, it must pass through the condition of the soul. Therefore, unresolved damage, bitterness, shame, or false structure can muddy what God is trying to express through a person.

The Logos Restores Order

A governing idea in the book. Christ as the Logos does not merely inspire. He reorganizes what false systems, damage, and contradiction threw out of rank.

The Soul Cannot Heal While Holding Debt

A foundational forgiveness principle in the book. Unforgiveness keeps the inner life cold, preserves accusation, and blocks restored feeling.

Theology of Exposure

God exposes to heal, not to shame. In this framework, divine exposure is mercy because it breaks secrecy and gives truth access to the real wound.

What Hell Numbs, the Holy Ghost Must Awaken

A book phrase describing the need for visitation and awakening where darkness has made the soul dull. In this book, numbness is not solved by better management but by the Shepherd restoring the soul.

What You Hide, You Hand to Darkness

A governing restoration principle. Hidden things remain outside the hand of remedy. In this book, what is concealed stays untreated, but what comes to light can come under the hand of God.

Wholeness

A condition in which the inward life has come back under God's order. In this book, wholeness is more than symptom management, emotional relief, or functional religion. It is healed order.

Wrong Feels Normal

A condition in which repeated exposure to darkness, bondage, confusion, or dysfunction weakens the soul's alarm system. In this book, when wrong feels normal, the soul is already wounded and must be remeasured by Kingdom normal.

Thematic Word Index

206, 207, 215, 233, 239,
252, 265, 272, 276, 279

Scripture Index

Other Good Books
from EKI Publishing

www.ekibooks.com

- *The Unique Factor*
    - By David Webb
- *Escape the Shame of Babylon*
    - By David Webb
- *Building the Kingdom Through the Local Church*
    - By David Webb
- *Building the Temple to Hold the Glory*
    - By David Webb
- *Soul Made Whole*
    - By David Webb
- *Unchained: Freed to be His Treasure*
    - By Kirkland M. Rite
- *Baptized: Why did I get Wet*
    - By Kirland M. Rite
- *Sozo: What Am I Saved From?*
    - By Kirland M. Rite
- *Covenant of Salt: The Gospel and a Pretzel*
    - By Kirland M. Rite

Coming from Eternal Kingdom International Publishing

2026

Covenant of Salt
By Kirkland M. Rite

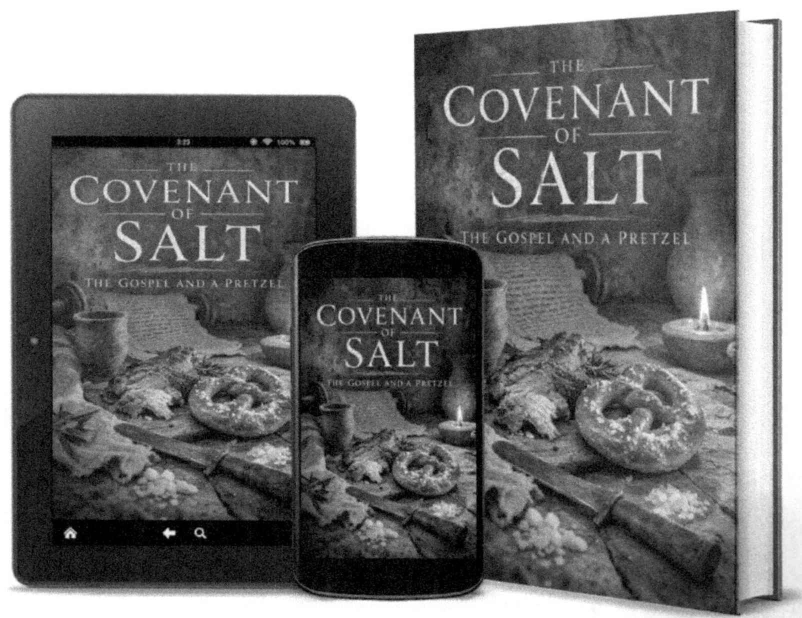

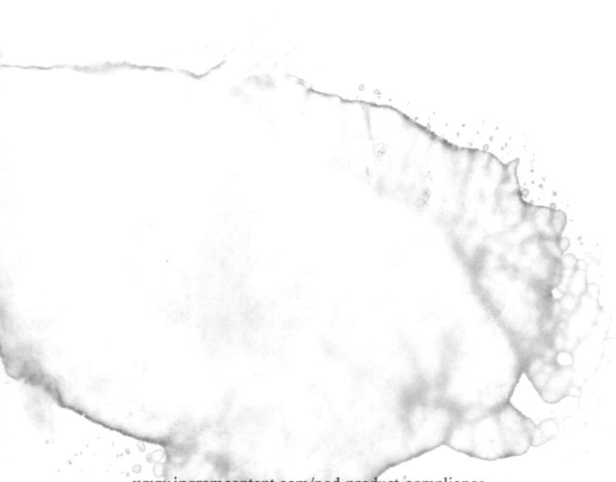

www.ingramcontent.com/pod-product-compliance
Lightning Source LLC
Chambersburg PA
CBHW051507050726

47594CB00010B/3994